MW00666962

NOTICE TO READER

ISBN 0-9680600-0-5

The Easy Résumé Book may be purchased through:

Bowes
Leadership Group

Suite 303 – 35 King Street
Winnipeg, Manitoba, Canada
R3B 1H4
Phone: (204) 947-5525
Email: bjb@bowesgroup.com

Table of Contents

About the Author

Barbara J. Bowes
C.M.C., C.H.R.P., M.Ed.

Barbara J. Bowes is a well-known Manitoba management consultant and President of Bowes Leadership Group, Inc. a fast growing professional services firm. Barbara is a certified management consultant and certified human resource management professional with university degrees in cross-cultural education, learning disabilities and a graduate degree in administration. Barbara is also a popular public speaker and workshop leader. Barbara was awarded 1990 Woman of the Year (Manitoba) for her leadership and dedication to aspiring young career professionals and for her assistance for women re-entering the workforce. She is listed in the World's Whose Who of Women 1993 and was nominated three times as Instructor of the Year by her students at the University of Manitoba. For the last several years she has been teaching her résumé methodology to both clients and professionals through her professional career transition services.

Barbara designed the transferable skills or competency based résumé methodology early in her career when she realized that she had the expertise but not the experience to take on higher-level career positions. Barbara was adamant that she could demonstrate her skills and thus analyzed her various roles, responsibilities and tasks. Identifying what she was really good at and what she liked to do, she then designed her résumé methodology so that the employer would focus on these skills and not her job titles.

Barbara's lifelong focus on skills and competencies has enabled her to undertake many career challenges. Her work has taken her to the field of social work, public education, university instruction, not-for-profit executive management, and school trusteeship. Today she runs a successful and growing management consulting practice providing services in executive search, career transition, performance coaching, training and development, organization design and general operations management.

Acknowledgments

Although I consider myself rather tenacious, I can only say that persistent pushing by friends, colleagues and especially clients was critical to starting and completing the task of compiling this book. While I had been teaching my methodology for many, many years, I had never taken the time to formalize it into a book. It has been a daunting task and has given me a far greater appreciation of the whole book writing, publishing and distribution business.

My clients and other professionals tell me that they find this methodology works for anyone, it is inspiring and uplifting and it seems to be able to create a strong new sense of self-confidence that appeals to employers and results in jobs. ***Hooray!*** So it is with great thanks that I recognize the long line of support from all of my customers, career transition specialists, high school teachers and students, aspiring professionals, career questers and others who have given me encouragement over the years.

Introduction

Why Write Another Book on How to Write a Résumé!?!

There are a great many résumé books on the market, so why write another one?

The answer is simple – most of these résumé books are confusing; they tell you all about the different kinds of résumés, but, by the end of the book, you still don't know which one to use and you are more frustrated than ever. This book is about one, and only one, résumé style. I call it the **Transferable Skills** Résumé because it identifies your key skills or competencies and aids you in portraying these competencies in the most positive way.

The Transferable Skills, or Competency Résumé, helps you to get your next job based on the skills you have to offer, not **where** you got your skills or **how** you got your skills.

It will help you to manage trouble spots such as an outdated educational background or the lack of formal education. It also helps those individuals who have much to offer because of their lifetime of experience in the "school of hard knocks", but who don't know how to state these skills to their advantage in a résumé.

It is a résumé style that encourages you to be creative. You are encouraged to place the different informational pieces where they sell you the most. The résumé becomes your personal masterpiece and concentrates on selling and marketing your special strengths.

I have been using this résumé style for over 15 years. I designed it before competencies were popular. I did it because I needed a way to demonstrate that I could do a job that I was applying for even though I didn't have direct, "hands on" experience. I have taught it to individuals at all levels of the career ladder and to individuals coming from business, industry, public sector, non-profit, university and women re-entering the workforce. The response has been overwhelmingly positive.

People who have used this résumé style have been overjoyed by their success. Why? **Because people get interviews and people get jobs!** Not only that; their self-esteem soars sky high!

Over the years, many of my clients have not only suggested, but have begged me to write a book. The first book was published in 1995. We have sold over 12,000 books and this is our 3rd edition. We hope it will bring you success too!

How is This Book Different From the Rest?

This book is unique because it not only gives you a practical and easy method to identify your skills or competencies and to format your résumé, it provides you with comprehensive resource lists to help you put your thoughts on paper.

You will find lists that help you to describe your personal traits and your preferred working environment, as well as extensive competency statements for the most common skills. There are samples of personal profiles for a number of careers and a series of accomplishments for each and, finally, a sampling of completed résumés for your reference.

The comprehensive lists in this book have been compiled from real life examples – from clients who have used this résumé style to successfully reposition themselves in the career market place.

Describing your strengths and your general skills is hard work. Not everyone has the mastery of words required to write a good résumé. This book is your resource. The comprehensive lists it contains have been compiled from real life examples – from clients who have used this résumé style to successfully reposition themselves in the career market place. Use this book just like you would a dictionary or a resource book.

Create your own dynamic résumé. As the author, I give you permission to copy the working charts in this workbook. You'll need several pages so be prepared. By the end of all your thinking, reading, remembering, blood, sweat and tears, you will have a well-developed résumé. Your résumé will be a concise summary of all your key strengths and skills. Your résumé will be a cut above the rest and your name will appear on that sacred interview short list.

Because the work history and career of every person is unique, it is hard to write a résumé book that will address all of the issues of its readers. However, I have shared as many special tips with you as I can. You will see these special tips all throughout the book.

Finally, this résumé book will teach you to use the dynamics of psychology to make a strong visual presentation that GETS INTERVIEWS AND GETS JOBS.

GOOD LUCK!

What Is A Transferable Skills Résumé?

A transferable skills résumé highlights your strengths through the use of key competency summaries.

The whole résumé is focused on your key compentencies.
I am not interested so much in where you developed these skills, how you developed them or when you developed them. I want to see a résumé that focuses on what you can do – your key compentencies.

Key skills are what the first page of your résumé is all about. By identifying your skills and showcasing them on the first page of your résumé, you allow the employer to read about your skills and to quickly see how these skills can be used in the job they are recruiting for. This presentation of key skills will help you to pass that 10 second acid test that all résumés have to go through in order to be placed on the "look at again" pile.

How Will The Transferable Skills Résumé Benefit You?

The transferable skills résumé is so successful because it saves the reader (hopefully your next employer) a great deal of time and energy. The reader does not have to spend time trying to figure out, from your duties and responsibilities, just what skills you have. They can see the skills listed on the front page!

What Are Other Reasons That The Transferable Skills Résumé Works so Well?

- It identifies the skills used/developed from each of your jobs. It gives you a solid knowledge of what you can do and helps to increase your self-esteem. After all, you have taken yourself for granted for too long.
- The solid knowledge and confidence it gives helps you to present yourself in a confident manner in an interview. You don't have to think on your feet about your strengths and your weaknesses, you have already explored these and understand them well.
- It helps you to understand which skills you like or dislike using and the skills you really want to use in your next new job.
- It helps you to see where you can use your skills in any job market sector. This is becoming very important because of the trends toward multi-skilling of employees and the need or desire to take a job in a different business sector.
- It presents all of your skills together, rather than scattered throughout the résumé. There is no second guessing or flipping pages.
- It will highlight what you can do instead of emphasizing your previous duties, your previous employer, or your level of education.

- It has proven to be very effective for people who have changed jobs over the years and for people who have had only one job in their career.
- It can be very effective for new graduates who have more knowledge than practical skills or for women re-entering the workforce who have gained skills from their work in the home and in the community.

A Before and After View

If you are not convinced that the Transferable Skills Résumé is for you, then perhaps a look at a sample résumé showing a before and after view will convince you.

The before view is typical of résumés that cross my desk. It does not sell the candidate well.

The after view using the transferable skills format, features WHO YOU ARE and WHAT YOU CAN DO – all on page one. The reader will see if your skills are what they are looking for with ease. It saves the employer time and you will get that all important interview.

So let's get started.

Before

CURRICULUM VITAE

Joyce Gee
178 Irish Avenue
Winnipeg, Manitoba
R2G 1J3
555–6681(Home) 555–6677(Fax)

PROFILE:

- Has seven years experience in all aspects of non-profit human service organization including but not limited to: Board development and liaison; community and external relations; Administration and management of personnel, finance, administrative and program.
- Knowledge of the principles, practices, methods, techniques and objectives of social planning and community development work.
- Exhibits high degree of professionalism.
- Superior communication skills.
- Broad managerial skills.
- Demonstrated awareness and sensitivity to health and social service issues.
- Knowledge of political, health care, social service agencies and systems.
- Proficient networking experience at various levels of agencies and systems.
- Has experience in public relations.
- Strong belief in community participation and community directed programming.
- Strong analytical skills.
- Ability to relate to senior levels of business, governmental agencies, the medical professions as well as other organizations.
- Knowledge of community development work and citizen participation methods and techniques.

DEMONSTRATED PROFICIENCY IN:

Administrative and Organizational Skills:

- Substantial understanding of the fundamentals of not-for-profit management.
- Responsible for budget development and control of resources for an annual budget in excess of $500,000.
- Responsible for a staff of 15 and a volunteer component of 30.
- Assumed chief responsibilities for: public accountability of funds; maintenance of agency systems and controls; and development of policies and procedures.
- Planning and facilitating community consultations.
- Organization and direction of several simultaneous projects.
- Creative problem solving.

Communication and Human Relation Skills:

- Excellent interpersonal skills.
- Preparation of and conducting all aspects of press conferences.
- Public Relations and interviews with the media.
- Personnel Development.
- Liaison with Federal, Provincial and Municipal departments including politicians.
- Knowledge of human rights legislation and employment standards.
- Demonstrated ability to bring various key actors together.
- Group facilitation including: conducting workshops and training programs on topical issues [domestic violence, poverty, housing, health and social justice issues] for professionals, community groups, government commissions and educational institutions.

EDUCATION:

1987	Health Care Management Certificate; Assiniboine Community College.
1977	Certificate of Elementary Education; Brandon University, Brandon.
1976	Bachelor of Arts (Major-Psychology, Minor-Athletic & Recreation Studies); University of Winnipeg.
1973	Grade 12 Diploma; Rural Collegiate; Rural, Manitoba.

CONTINUING EDUCATION:

1986–1994 Board Development: Manitoba Committee on Wife Abuse, Winnipeg West Child and Family Services, Association of Child and Family Service Agencies, Westborne Housing Co-op, Manitoba Health Organizations, Manitoba Public Health Association, Manitoba Association of Community Health Centres. Attended conferences and workshops dealing with various aspects of Boards [structure, process, policy and procedure].

1986–1994 Staff Development: Dauphin Crisis Centre, Social Planning Council and Hope Centre Health Care Inc.

1992 Managing the Non-Profit Organization: Manitoba Institute of Management, Winnipeg.

1986–1988 Supervisors' Training: Province of Manitoba, Education and Training, New Careers Program. [Several three day sessions providing employee supervision techniques].

1986–1987 Group Facilitation Training, Chemical Dependency Intervention Course, Diffusing Hostility, Treatment of Child Sexual Abuse, Domestic Abuse Project Workshop on Women's Support Groups, Current Issues in Chemical Dependency.

EMPLOYMENT HISTORY:

1990–1994 Executive Director
North End Community Health Centre Inc.
As Chief Executive Officer responsible for the overall program management and services; administration and financial management; interpretation and implementation of policies and programs as instituted by the Board of Directors; with accountability to the Board of Directors.
Reason for leaving: Termination of contract.

1989–1990 Social Planner
Planning Council
As a social planner responsible for social planning, social policy analysis, consultation and community education activities. Also provided social planning information and assistance to members, staff, Board of Directors, various committees and interest groups who dealt with social services, educational and health services.
Reason for leaving: Left for new position.

1988–1989	Winnipeg West Child and Family Services – Program Committee Chair
1989–1990	Winnipeg West Child and Family Services – Board of Directors Chairperson Manitoba Association of Child and Family Service Agencies Vice-Chair
1988	Children's Foundation Board of Directors – Member Westboine Housing Co-op Board of Directors – Member
1986–1988	M.C.W.A. Board of Directors Parkland Representative M.C.W.A. Board of Directors Vice-Chairperson
1986–1987	Crime Prevention Committee – Member Suicide Prevention Committee – Member
1985–1987	Sunday School Assistant Superintendent Sunday School Support Team Moms and Tots – Founding Member

After

Joyce Gee B.A., C.H.C.M.

178 Irish Avenue
Winnipeg, Manitoba R2G 1J3

Phone: (204) 555–6681
Fax: (204) 555–6677

Authentic, self-motivated, astute professional specializing in organizational and community development. Committed to integrity. Key strengths in problem solving, interpersonal communications and outstanding skills in the analyzing, assessing and prioritizing of information. Proven ability to liaise and network at all levels of the system. Effectively addresses advocacy issues with a humanistic approach. Committed to contributing to the growth and efficiency of an organization. Seeking a challenging opportunity to use my unique set of skills and expertise.

PROFESSIONAL EXPERTISE

- Excellent **Organizational and Planning Strengths** for human service sector organization including policy and program design, development, implementation and evaluation.
- Exceptional **Interpersonal and Communication Skills** with the ability to work with people at various levels in the organizational structure, sensitive to individual needs relative to team process, and the goals of the organization.
- Natural **Leadership** ability with key strengths in delegating, coordinating and organizing people, information and tasks.
- **Managed** the coordination of organization administration, financial and human resources systems.
- Creative and innovative **Trainer and Facilitator** with experience in research, needs assessment, design, development and evaluation of customized programs.
- Empathic **Listener** with an intuitive ability to counsel individuals.
- Strong belief in win/win **Negotiation** process for agreement and understanding.
- Solid knowledge of **Team Dynamics** with keen sensitivity to team members.
- **Written communication skills** for the preparation and submission of presentations/briefs to funding agencies, hearings and task forces.
- **Committed** to being on the leading edge, the mastery of new skills and knowledge.

PROFESSIONAL ACCOMPLISHMENTS

- Managed a team of multi-disciplinary professionals to develop and deliver comprehensive programs and services based on community development model.
- Instrumental in developing Agency network with a broad cross-section of the human service sector – social service, health care, education, multi-cultural, recreation and employment and training at all levels – program, management, governance, government and political.
- Designed, developed and presented workshops on domestic violence to law enforcement agencies, health care professionals, armed forces, community groups, and church groups.
- Designed, developed and facilitated a seminar on " Emotional Abuse in the Workplace" for the Human Resource Certificate Program, Continuing Education Program University of Manitoba and workshops on community development to New Careers Department of Education and Continuing Education, University of Manitoba.
- Designed, developed and facilitated training of volunteer crisis counsellors and various workshops on interpersonal relationships and personal growth issues.
- Ensured Agency operated on a balanced budget by organizing, coordinating and directing operations within the budgeting environment.
- Responsible for initiating establishment of and ensuring maintenance of Agency reporting and control systems in the areas of human resource management, financial and administrative.
- Generated parameters of Agency Policy and Procedure Manual – developed and coordinated appropriate policies; implemented and monitored the policies.

EDUCATION

Bachelor of Arts (Psychology & Recreation Studies), University of Winnipeg
Certificate in Elementary Education, Brandon University
Certificate in Health Care Management, Assiniboine Community College

PROFESSIONAL DEVELOPMENT (abbreviated)

Business Management Forum, Federal Business Development Bank 1995
First Responders Course, 1994
Board Development: (involvement on behalf of seven organizations), 1986–1994
Manitoba Institute of Management, Managing the Non-Profit Organization, Winnipeg 1992
Supervisors' Training, New Careers Education and Training 1986–1988
Professional Development Courses on topics ranging from Group Facilitation
to Chemical Dependency, 1985–1994

EMPLOYMENT HISTORY

Executive Director	North End Community Health Centre
Social Planner	Planning Council
Assistant Executive Director	Provincial Committee on Family Violence
Director	Rural Crisis Centre

PROFESSIONAL LEADERSHIP (abbreviated)

Co-chair Healthy Public Policy, Manitoba Public Health Association, 1994–1995
Member, Winnipeg Child and Family Services Northwest Area Council 1994–1995
Member, Urban Health Advisory Council Member 1993–1994
Member, Manitoba Health Organizations Board of Directors 1992–1994
Co-Chair, North End Housing Project 1993–1994
Member Steering Committee, Natl Community Health Centre Conference 1992–1993
Member Board of Directors, MB Association of Community Health Centres 1990–1994
Chair, Interagency Urban Futures 1990–1992
Chairperson Board of Directors, Winnipeg West Child and Family Services 1990–1991
Vice-Chair Board of Directors, Manitoba Association of Child and Family Services 1989–1990
Founding Member, Children's Foundation Board of Directors 1989–1990
Vice-Chair Board of Directors, M.C.W.A., 1988–1989

PRESENTATIONS AND PUBLICATIONS

Aboriginal Justice Inquiry – prepared paper for submission 1989
Royal Commission on Violence Against Women – prepared paper for presentation 1992
National Conference on Community Health Centres – Workshop presenter 1994
Manitoba Health Organizations Annual Conference – Workshop presenter 1994

Let's Get Started

Researching, preparing for and writing your résumé will not be easy. It will take a good solid effort on your part. The résumé is really an in-depth exploration of yourself and your work. You will have to look very closely at yourself. This requires personal honesty and persistence. If you work steadily on a full time basis, you might have a first draft in two days. If you are working on the résumé part-time, then give yourself at least one week of working every night.

The steps that you take to create your résumé are systematic and will build on each other as you continue toward the goal. It may appear that we are tackling this project backwards but we are really asking you to do the easy work first. The steps that you will follow are outlined below:

The Twelve Steps to Building Your Résumé

Assessing Yourself

1. Assessing and documenting work history
2. Identifying your preferred work environment
3. Assessing and documenting education and professional development
4. Assessing and documenting professional leadership
5. Identifying the job duties in each job – what did you do?
6. Assessing how you carried out these duties
7. Assessing what skills you needed to carried out the duties
8. Categorizing and classifying the skills and identifying likes and dislikes

Building The Résumé

9. Choosing action words, power words and power phrases
10. Building your key skills phrases
11. Building your accomplishments
12. Building and finalizing your résumé

Steps one through eight will be repeated with every job (paid or non-paid) that you have had so prepare yourself with extra paper and be prepared for a whole lot of work.

ALRIGHT, LET'S REALLY GET TO WORK

Assessing and Documenting Work History

The first step in building the skills résumé is to assess your work history. The work history assessment includes an examination of all your job titles, all of the activities that make up these jobs, as well as looking at the working environment that surrounds them. It also includes any special achievements and accomplishments that you can identify.

The purpose of the work history assessment is to find out what jobs you have worked in over your career. You want to look at job titles, industries, dates and reasons for leaving. This will immediately help you to see if you can categorize the industries that you have worked in or if the titles of jobs you held years ago are still valid. Of course, we will also find out that company name changes have occurred and our references are no longer available. That's OK. This is simply the documentation section to help you identify problems.

You may be worried as you start this exercise that you have changed jobs frequently or on the other hand, you may be worried that you have only had one job. **PLEASE DO NOT WORRY.** Remember, the information developed from this assessment is for your eyes only. It will alert you to glaring **holes** in your experience that will be addressed later. It is simply important that you write everything down. Later on, you will use your good judgement to choose the specific information that you want when it comes time to finalize your résumé.

The work history assessment includes a summary of all of the jobs you have held in your career; it also includes reasons for leaving. This is included on your worksheets so that you will have brought the reasons forward into your memory. You will not include it in the résumé. It is helpful to you because you are reminded of exactly why you left a job. Believe me, you may very well be asked that question in your interview and you must be prepared to answer it. The person that will make the best impression is the one who has a ready made answer for this question rather than the person who has to think of why they left a job right in the middle of the interview. Also, if the reason might bring you difficulty in an interview, you want to prepare for it. So, be sure to list the reason for leaving your jobs.

Fill out the Work History Assessment List

Start by filling out the work history list. Continue making a list on your own paper if you run out of room. Remember, you want to develop your work history information as completely as possible but you will only be using part of it in your final résumé. The unused information will be kept on hand for further reference and if required it will be easy to put into an updated or revised résumé.

Begin with your most recent work/position. Try to keep a timeframe of 10 years in mind. Describe all of the jobs over the 10 year period. For any job older than 10 years, you must ask yourself – **does this job add value to your present career direction?** If so, then complete the information.

We have provided an example for you. Please feel free to copy extra pages as you need them.

Examples

POSITION TITLE	Administrative Manager
PLACE OF EMPLOYMENT	Calmar Manufacturing
ADDRESS	London, Ontario
DATES OF EMPLOYMENT	1977 – 1990
REASON FOR LEAVING	Laid off (economic-recession)
REFERENCES AVAILABLE	Yes, favourable, would need forwarding address of supervisor

Notes

Under this section, write anything that comes to mind that you might want to look at again. For instance, did you solve any special problems that you could use in the discussion of accomplishments? Write a few notes just to jog your memory.

Work History Assessment Sheet

POSITION TITLE:

PLACE OF EMPLOYMENT:

ADDRESS (CITY, PROVINCE):

DATES OF EMPLOYMENT:

REASON FOR LEAVING:

REFERENCE INFORMATION:

NOTES:

Transfer to your résumé

Formatting The Work History Summary

Now that you have completed your work history assessment, you are ready to transfer this information to the résumé. For the purposes of your draft résumé, use a separate sheet of paper for each résumé section. Once completed, keep it so that you can integrate it into the rest of the résumé.

The transferable résumé style also has another unique feature – it follows the way we read (i.e., from left to right). Therefore, wherever possible, critical information is put on the left so that we see it first and it stands out. List the titles of your job on the left, then the name of your company, with the dates. Use capital letters and bold print as shown in the example. When you have completed the entire résumé, you must go back and decide what type of font is best to use. It doesn't matter, as long as it has a pleasing visual effect on the reader.

Example One

WORK HISTORY

ADMINISTRATOR, Finance Department, McLeod Construction, 1984 – present

ACCOUNTING CLERK, Finance Department, Mars Plastics, 1980 – 1984

Tips For Formatting Your Work History

Every person is unique and has their own unique set of circumstances that are sometimes hard to translate into a résumé. The following tips will help you get over some of these rough spots.

- If you have always lived and worked in one location, then to restate this location; i.e., Winnipeg, is redundant and boring. Eliminate the location all together.
- If you are still in your current job, you can use the word *present* instead of a date.
- We often find that our job title changes over time but that the actual duties do not. If this is the case, then put the current job title, but include all the other titles in brackets so that you can easily refer to them. Then, when you finalize the résumé, decide which title to use. Use only one title; the preference is for the current title.
- If the job responsibilities changed as well as the title, you may well decide to state this as another job. Do so if you believe that it is distinct enough. It does not matter at this stage because you will be selective in your final draft of the résumé.

Remember: You are the product!

The most common mistake that people make when they do their résumé, is to highlight – usually in bold print and capital letters – the name of their former company! Ask yourself – who are you trying to sell with your résumé? Your former company or yourself? Remember: you are the product!

- There are times when your job title is so specialized that it does not mean very much in the general market. If this is the case, you should look for a parallel title that you might possibly use. Put this title in brackets near your original title. You can decide which one to use at a later time.
- One problem that often arises is the dates and months of the year that you began or ended a job. A good approach to that problem is this: if the job is six months or less, then include the months; if the job is more than six months then use only the year. For example: January – April 1981 (less than six months).
- Summer employment and part time employment can be a problem when trying to describe this on a résumé. For instance, if you worked at the same summer job for three summers, you could write the description like this:

SURVEYOR ASSISTANT, Bowman Construction, 1988–1990, Summer Employment

- If you held the same kind of job but with different companies you could state the industry rather that a specific company.

TRADES HELPER, Construction Industry, 1991–1993

- The same problem can arise for those who have had full time, regular part time jobs or casual positions for a time. In this situation put the titles all on one line. Example:

HEALTH CARE AIDE, Dysan Centre Hospital, 1977 – 1990, Regular, part-time, casual

- In some cases people act in a more senior position on a temporary basis. These acting positions are usually of short duration but the employee can take an acting position several times during one working year or within the career time frame. It is difficult to advise on this problem in a general sense but there are a few ways that this can be handled. If you have had a number of acting positions that represent a promotion over the years of your employment, you can isolate this as a "new" job. For instance, a leadhand in a manufacturing plant who was acting in the foreman position for periods of three to six months at a time over several years, may be able to state this higher level of employment in this manner:

ACTING FOREMAN, Carmel Manufacturing, Winnipeg, Manitoba, January – October, 1989

- If you have been out of work for some time, you have to find some way to explain what you have been doing. If you have been doing contract or consulting work then use the terms contractor or consultant.

CONSULTANT/INDEPENDENT CONTRACTOR	Lincoln Manufacturing, 1995 – present

You have now completed the basic work experience outline. You have written it on a separate piece of paper. You will decide later just where to place it on your résumé.

Identifying Your Preferred Work Environment

You have now completed your work history assessment and you have confirmed where you worked and what jobs you worked in. Now is the time to ask yourself – what did I like (or not like) about each work environment? Review the **notes** section of your work history documents to see if you jotted down any information that can be helpful here.

Jot a few answers to the following questions in the note spaces provided. Confirm with yourself:

What did you like about working at each job?

Would you want to work in that kind of work environment again?

If you need help with any ideas, refer to the section Work Environment Phrases, Page 75 to find descriptors that might assist you.

Assessing and Documenting Education and Professional Development

Now it is time to look at your qualifications in the areas of formal education or professional development. Once again, for the purpose of the draft résumé, use a clean sheet of paper for this section. The rough draft will list all your formal education and your professional development. When this is done, decide what order to put it and where in the résumé to insert it.

Formal Education – means a degree, certificate or diploma that you received from a recognized educational institution.

Professional Development – is any course or workshop that you have taken to upgrade your skills. Courses can be one day to several weeks in length and can be offered by a professional association or through a professional training businesses such as the Canadian Management Association. A certificate can be obtained for some professional development courses – you will have to decide if you will use it on the résumé.

Write these qualifications in any order – just get them written down. Then follow the instructions for organizing and prioritizing your list.

Organizing And Prioritizing Your List

Once you have listed your formal education and/or professional development qualifications, ask the following questions to help you prioritize the list.

- What kind of education do you have? Is there more formal education than informal professional development?
- What is more current, your formal education or professional development? Depending on the number of courses/programs/ certificates, try putting the most current formal education first.
- What sells you the best – your formal education or your professional development? Choose what ever sells you the best and list this first.
- Is your formal education from Canada or from another country? Is your education recognized or reputable? You will want to include your education but displaying your professional development first may sell you the best.

- Review your list for visual effectiveness. Use bold or italic fonts or create two lists separated by a space. Move these résumé pieces around until you are satisfied that it gives a strong position statement about the qualifications you offer.

Formatting Your Education And Professional Development History

As you will see from the following example, there are three sections – formal degrees, formal certificates and professional development. As well, you should use the full name of your university. If it causes the date to run on the second line, then try to use the abbreviation as shown below.

Although the professional development in this example is more current, the sample candidate felt that the academic degrees were more important. In this case, it was also felt that there was additional credibility given by adding who sponsored the professional development courses. Depending on the number of courses, this may be optional because it tends to make the résumé look visually crowded.

MASTER OF EDUCATION, Personnel & Administration, U of M, 1987

BACHELOR OF EDUCATION, Secondary Studies, U of W, 1984

BACHELOR OF SCIENCE, U of W, 1983

Certificate, Administrative Leadership
Certificate, Special Education
Certificate, School Psychology

- *Managing Conflict in Today's Schools,* Dept. of Education, 1993
- *TQM in an Educational Environment,* M.T.S., 1993
- *Developing Positive Work & Home Relations,* Department of Education, 1993

If you have a long list of professional development workshops, then review the list and select only the most current (i.e., last 5 years) or make your selection based on any other appropriate criteria. The résumé must be visually balanced as well, so if your list simply looks too long, reduce the size of the list.

There will be times when you feel your professional development is not only more current but also more relevant than a degree. In that case, put professional development as the lead statement.

Tips For Formatting The Education/Professional Development History

Once again, every person will have a unique problem when it comes to trying to state education and professional development qualifications. The following tips may be helpful but it must be emphasized again – **What adds value? What sells you the best?** Only you can decide.

Reminder

Rewrite your educational/professional development qualifications on a separate sheet of paper. Save it to integrate with the rest of the résumé.

- You can make the decision on whether to include dates or not. If the topic is more influential than the date then exclude the date. If including dates makes one or two of your courses look too outdated, then either don't use dates at all or use only current dates for the first three or so of your list.
- If you do not have a degree or certificate, then leave education out and only use the title professional development.
- If you only have one or two courses and they are somewhat outdated, then leave the section on professional development out of the résumé.
- If you have neither an education or professional development that would add a positive tone to the résumé, then leave the whole section out. Of course, you'll have to make up for this with all of your work accomplishments!

Assessing Community/Professional Leadership

The next section of the résumé will help show your initiative and leadership accomplishments in either your community or in your profession. It includes all volunteer work, whether it is for your church, volunteer in a seniors home, for your community club or for a professional association.

Write your community/professional leadership jobs in the same manner as you did with your paid jobs. Make copies of the worksheet provided for you.

Community/Professional Leadership Worksheet

POSITION TITLE:

NAME OF ORGANIZATION:

DATES:

RESPONSIBILITIES:

SPECIAL PROBLEMS/PROJECTS:

NOTES:

What did you like about this work environment?

Tips For Formatting The Community/Professional Leadership History

- Once you make your list, decide if you have more community versus professional leadership. This will determine which title to put first. If you only want to use one title that's fine. You can use bold caps, similar to your jobs sheet or bold italics or plain italics. Try out different fonts – remember, visual impression is important.
- If you do not have any volunteer experiences, then leave this section out. If you have only one or two statements for this section, you will have to decide if they add any value to your résumé.

Formatting The Community/Professional Leadership History

PROFESSIONAL/COMMUNITY LEADERSHIP

Reminder

Rewrite your community and professional leadership qualifications on a separate sheet of paper. Save it to integrate with the rest of your résumé.

In this example, the candidate chose to separate the professional volunteer service from the community service, because the employer to whom they were applying would more greatly appreciate the professional leadership. Depending on the length of the lists, you might also choose to use bold capital letters or lowercase bold italics. Sometimes you have had several leadership positions with one organization; if you have three or less, list them as in the example above, if you have more, then you will have to carefully assess the visual effects of repeating the one organization too many times.

Chairperson, Saskatchewan Society of Engineering Technologists
Treasurer, Saskatchewan Society of Engineering Technologists
Member, Saskatchewan Society of Engineering Technologists

Club Leader, Boyko Community College
President, Mystery Readers Association
Parent Volunteer, Readview Day Care Centre

You have now completed three sections of the résumé; work history, education/professional development and volunteer/professional leadership. The arrangement of the various sections on your résumé will depend on what sells you the best. There is no one right answer! Leave it until you have finished your skills analysis but do a first pass look and ask yourself what order would sell me the best?

These sections were the easy part of your résumé. Now you will move to the hard part – that of identifying your skills.

Your Skills Assessment

Most of us tend to think about our duties, in other words what tasks we did in our various work placements. For the transferable skills résumé you must think about how you carried out your tasks and what skills your tasks required. It is these skills and the sum of all the skills that you have acquired over your lifetime that will help you find another job.

So it is important to look carefully at every job or volunteer leadership position no matter how long ago. You need to look at all of your tasks no matter how trivial they appear. You need to identify all the skills you have developed whether they were gained through paid or unpaid work.

Let's begin.

Using An Assessment Framework

The key to the transferable skills résumé is to ask yourself: (1) what you did, (2) how you did it and (3) what skills were required?

Make a copy of the worksheet provided to help you identify these three key things. Fill out these worksheets for every job and volunteer position that you have had. Keep going until you have exhausted all of your ideas or at least until you start to see a pattern developing. Only then will you be ready to classify and categorize these skills.

A number of examples have been done for you. The examples demonstrate that this assessment tool can easily be used in any paid or non-paid work situation. Then, you will see a blank worksheet for your own use. Make yourself several copies.

Worksheet

JOB TITLE/POSITION: Manager

WHAT DID I DO?	HOW DID I DO IT?	WHAT SKILLS DID I USE?
• corporate budgets • treasury • financial planning	• consolidated 7 divisions • solid financial skills • project leadership	• communication • strategic planning • co-ordination

JOB – TITLE/POSITION: Volunteer Co-ordinator

COMPANY NAME: Local Community Club

WHAT DID I DO?	HOW DID I DO IT?	WHAT SKILLS DID I USE?
• organized annual banquet	• called parents and asked for volunteers and donations • selected time, location • got notices ready • made arrangements for entertainment	• interpersonal communication • co-ordination • planning • scheduling

JOB TITLE/POSITION: Computer Systems Administrator

WHAT DID I DO?	HOW DID I DO IT?	WHAT SKILLS DID I USE?
• provided technical support and maintenance services • ensured data integrity and long term storage	• responded to calls on a timely basis • learned the design of the company systems • participated in the setting of policies and procedures	• technical proficiency in hardware platforms and a large variety of software applications • ability to learn new technologies quickly • skilled in translating and simplifying technical concepts to end users • good detail orientation and project management skills

JOB TITLE/POSITION: Receptionist

WHAT DID I DO?	HOW DID I DO IT?	WHAT SKILLS DID I USE?
• received incoming mail • received phone calls • confidential correspondence	• date stamped, sorted, prioritized • screened calls, took messages • keyboarding/WordPerfect • computer skills • confidentiality • communication	• organizational skills • customer service • tact and diplomacy

JOB TITLE/POSITION: Homemaker

WHAT DID I DO?	HOW DID I DO IT?	WHAT SKILLS DID I USE?
• raised three kids • worked on farm • led volunteer women's group	• developed and managed three personalities • read parenting books • sewed clothing • cooking, canning • gardening • budgeting • reading to children • tutoring/homework	• communication • humour • create own pattern • follow detailed pattern • creativity • following directions • managing a budget • organizing • co-ordinating • problem solving

JOB TITLE/POSITION: High School Grad – School Studies

WHAT DID I DO?	HOW DID I DO IT?	WHAT SKILLS DID I USE?
• studied seven subjects • wrote essays, exams, did projects	• developed a study schedule and followed it • located and did research on topics • used the computer	• organization and co-ordination skills • self-discipline, time management • responsibility • writing, editing skills • research and analysis • ability to work independently and on a team

Skills Assessment Worksheet

JOB – TITLE/POSITION ______________________

COMPANY/ORGANIZATION NAME ______________________

WHAT DID I DO?	HOW DID I DO IT?	WHAT SKILLS DID I USE?

Summarizing Your Skills

You have now completed a skills worksheet for each paid or unpaid job. Hopefully you have started to see a pattern among your skills.

You are now ready to classify and categorize those skills. Look them over carefully. What do you see? Write all of the patterns down. To begin, simply create your summary list. Then ask yourself – can I categorize some of my skills? Look at the following example.

EXAMPLE

- technical skills – finance
- treasury
- accounting
- planning, organizing and co-ordinating
- supervising
- leadership
- analyzing, synthesizing
- teamwork

Your next step is to list and priorize your skills in the order that best markets you. Number them or rewrite them from highest priority (the skills you want to use in your next job) to the lowest priority (a skill you can do but don't particularly like and don't really want to do a lot of in your next job).

Formatting The Skill Building Statements

Through this skills assessment process you will have identified specific skills, clustered them together and prioritized them. Now is the time to create your skills statements. These skills statements will be set out in the résumé in the following manner. Note that the heading will be either Professional Expertise or Key Skills – whatever you feel comfortable with.

PROFESSIONAL EXPERTISE/KEY SKILLS

- Priority #1 Skill Statement
- Priority #2 Skill Statement
- Priority #3 Skill Statement
- Priority #4 Skill Statement
- Priority #5 Skill Statement

The résumé skill statements always start with a word that describes the strength of your skill. Use words such as significant, excellent, or well developed. The statement should describe the skills you have. Sometimes you can add a component that demonstrates what you can do with that skill. We have listed a sampling of skill statements for you.

Sample Skills Statements

- Excellent strategic organizational planning and co-ordination skills for project and program initiation, staffing, start up, implementation and timely completion with limited budgets and resources.
- Good supervisory strengths for staff management, delegation, supervision, training and conflict resolution.
- Good interpersonal and leadership skills for the facilitation of a positive team-oriented management style in both corporate and regional work environments.
- Corporate level financial and economic analysis skills complemented by experience in major acquisition, divestiture or capital expenditure decisions.
- Extensive and successful experience and expertise in financial resource acquisitions and management, equipment procurement and budget development.

Tips For Building Skills Statements

Choose the heading that you are comfortable with, either professional expertise or key skills.

Include no more than approximately seven to ten statements in your résumé . If you have more than ten statements, try to combine them to reduce the overall list. Do not overflow to the second page unless it is absolutely necessary.

Be careful with the descriptors (i.e., extensive, excellent, superior or good). Make sure that you can defend the mastery level that you say you have. Do not be repetitive.

Skill statements are often hard to write, therefore the beauty of this book is that the skills statements are done for you. You simply refer to a skill, read the list of skill statements and select the one that best suits you. Transfer this to your draft skills page.

The skills lists have been written in alphabetical order.

Make any other special changes that you want. These statements are simply frameworks from which to build your own statements. It is rarely that you can use exactly what is written. You must make them your own. After all, you will have to defend them in an interview.

The Personal Profile Summary

The next important part of the résumé is your summary profile. It is situated at the top of the résumé and is a synopsis of the skills you offer. Please note that we do not label it as summary or profile. The summary profile should not be written until you have confirmed all of your skills.

Three key things are included in the summary.

1. Who you are (personal style traits).
2. What key skills you have.
3. What you are looking for in a job match (This can sometimes be omitted).

The descriptors that are recommended in the summary are those that reinforce what the reader will see described under the key skills section. The idea is that in a 10 SECOND glance – the reader can see who you are, what key skills you have and what you want. This section usually requires a great deal of writing and rewriting. Don't be discouraged. Start broadly and keep working the words until they are as clear and succinct as they can be. This 10 second glance will cause the reader to set your résumé aside to read in greater depth at a later time.

Reminder

The idea is that in a **10 SECOND** glance – the reader can see who you are, what key skills you have and what you want.

Typically the summary is highlighted by using **bold** or ***bold italics***, to help catch the readers eye. Read the following example.

Sample Summary Profile

Results-oriented generalist with versatile experience in administration and human resource management, staff recruitment, selection and training. Strong interpersonal and communication skills. Well developed analytical, creative problem solving, and decision making capabilities. Easily adaptable to change with a willingness to learn new concepts and technology. Demonstrated ability to work both autonomously and as a team player. Built long term relationships of trust and respect.

To help build your summary profile, you can also refer to the section called Special Personal Descriptors pages 61 to 78. This provides you with short phrases that describe personal traits, abilities and work environment statements that can be easily incorporated into a personalized statement. To take the shortcut, simply refer to the sample list of fully developed profiles starting on page 79. The following page shows you an example of what a completed first page of the résumé looks like.

BARBARA J. BOWES

99-67th St. East,
Vancouver, BC
V6S 4W1

1-250-555-1212

Highly skilled manager of diverse organizational functions. Strategic planner who takes initiative and is innovative, creative, and meets goals. A leader who is a trainer, facilitator and team builder. Bottom line manager who increases productivity and organizational effectiveness. Highly organized with good communication and interpersonal skills.

PROFESSIONAL EXPERTISE

- Priority #1 Skill Statement
- Priority #2 Skill Statement
- Priority #3 Skill Statement
- Priority #4 Skill Statement
- Priority #5 Skill Statement

Identifying Accomplishments/Achievements

You have now completed page one of your résumé. The next step to building your résumé is to examine your accomplishments or achievements. These are then incorporated into page two of the résumé.

What are accomplishments? What are achievements? People are always confused about this. We seem to believe that the only achievements that count are the achievements of acquiring a $1 million or saving your company $1 million. This is not true! Let's look at what an achievement or accomplishment really is.

An achievement and an accomplishment are the same thing. It is a task that you completed or carried out successfully, or a task that you finished to your satisfaction. It is a problem that you solved that had a noticeable result or improvement. The problem can be simple or complex. When identifying problems or projects to use in the accomplishment section, list a large number of problems and then select one that demonstrates the largest number of your skills. Try to keep the accomplishment list to a summary of three major problems that best cover all of your skills. This makes it easier when you are in the interview as you can refer to the same problem or accomplishment more than once by expanding on certain components of the problems.

Using an Accomplishment/Achievement Assessment Framework

The best way to find out and to be certain that you identify your accomplishments is to take a problem solving approach. It works this way:

- Go back and look at a job duty or task.
- Ask yourself – what problem(s) did I face in carrying out this responsibility? List them.
- How did I solve this problem? What did I do?
- How well did my solution work? What was the result?
- Write up an accomplishment statement. Write the statement by incorporating the answers to the above question.

This method is outlined in a chart or framework. It will help you to identify the problems/tasks which led to your accomplishments. Copy the worksheet provided for you.

JOB DUTY/TASK	PROBLEM
• organize a fundraising event	• lack of volunteers
	SOLUTION
	• went to the local school and offered a reference to those students who helped in our campaign
	RESULT
	• a successful fund-raiser

ACCOMPLISHMENT STATEMENT

Overcame a lack of volunteers by offering an exchange to senior high school students resulting in a successful fundraising campaign of over $100,000.

Accomplishment Assessment Worksheet

JOB DUTY/TASK	PROBLEM
	SOLUTION
	RESULT

ACCOMPLISHMENT STATEMENT

Sample Accomplishments

Read the following sample accomplishment statements. Once you have written a few accomplishments and you understand the framework, then you may feel confident to let go of the chart and simply write the accomplishment freehand.

- Acted as a facilitator at conferences and designed and/or delivered training courses on such diverse subjects as sexual harassment, telephone systems, effects of technology on the work place, interview techniques and assertiveness training.
- Communicated effectively and diplomatically with professional colleagues and subordinates as an analyst and a director, as an intermediary for the executive, and as an advisor to boards and senior political officials.
- Developed strategic and operational plans, policies and procedures for the leadership and management of an organizational unit consisting of 40 departments, a staff complement of 535 and an enrollment of 4,000 full-time and 19,000 continuing education students.
- Enhanced institutional profile and recognition by ensuring the increase of accredited programs. Provided executive support for the achievement of national or provincial accreditation of 16 programs over a seven year time period.
- Established emergency policies and procedures for fire protection, electrical, fuel and vital services including fire fighting procedures, plans of action, co-ordination of plans, salvage procedures and contingency plans.
- Reviewed and critiqued strategic plans for numerous Crown corporations operating in the utility, government services, and commercial sectors including integrating the major facilities planning process for a large utility working with the President and a task force of representatives of the key functional areas.

Should you wish to refer to the list of comprehensive accomplishment examples, turn to page 105 and select one which suits you or use sections of the accomplishment statements to create your own.

Finalizing Your Résumé

Page One Is Critical

Now is the time to put all of the résumé pieces together. Remember page one is always the same – the summary and key skills. It looks like the example below.

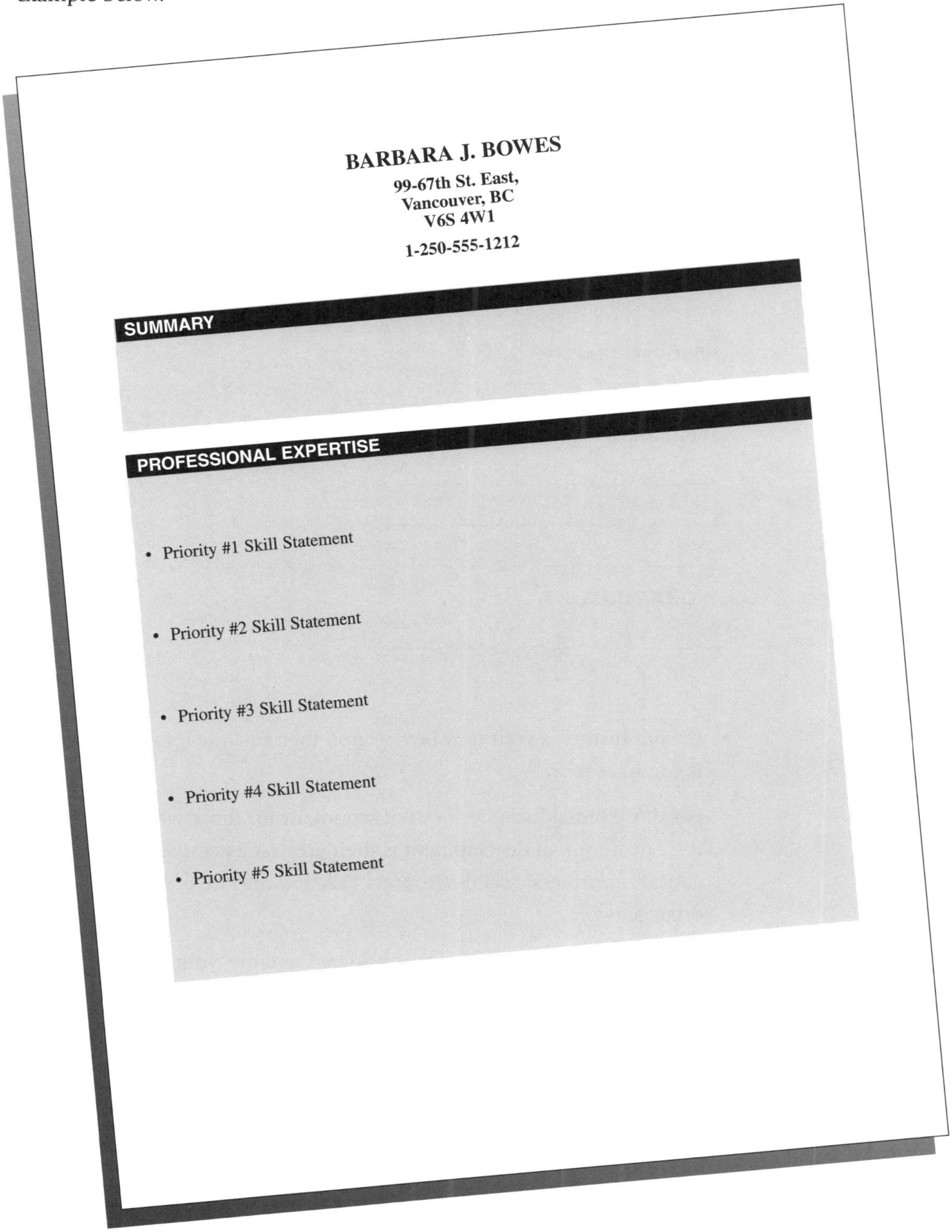

Tips For Selecting And Ordering Key Résumé Components

Page one – the statement of skills is compulsory. All other pages of your résumé are flexible and are dependent on what section sells you the best. Here are some tips to help you decide.

- Page arrangements can also be different depending on the length of information provided. You need to be careful with your list as it may appear overwhelming. A safe approach is to have one half of the page as accomplishments and the remainder displaying one or two other categories. It is important that you "play" with this to see what structure gives you the best visual image.

Example

ACCOMPLISHMENTS

- Accomplishments 1
- Accomplishments 2
- Accomplishments 3

PROFESSIONAL LEADERSHIP

_______ , _____________________

_______ , _____________________

_______ , _____________________

WORK HISTORY

_______ , _____________________

- If work history is your next best section then include it on page two if you have room.
- For those individuals fresh out of school, or for those who believe their professional development is their greatest asset, then the education/professional development section may be best placed on page two.
- For those individuals who are considered re-entry, your accomplishments in the voluntary sector might be appropriate or you may decide to display your volunteer leadership.
- The arrangement of all other sections following section one are your choice. Simply make sure you put your best features first.

The Finished Résumé

You have now finished your résumé. Remember, the only compulsory page format is page one. After that, it is you who decides what to place where. Keep in mind the question – **what sells you the best?**

Write your résumé on a word processor. Select the font and style that gives your résumé the best presence. Change from bold capital letters to italics or whatever will give you a good visual presentation.

Two complete sample résumés have been included for you. Although names and places are fictional, these résumés have been created by real individuals. Several additional examples are provided at the end of the book.

MELVIN A. LUCKY

163 Whitemouth Drive
Winnipeg, Manitoba
R6N 4E1

Res: (204) 555–1212

Effective, diplomatic management professional with proven administrative and financial skills; good abilities in oral and written communication; insightful problem solver; visionary.

PROFESSIONAL EXPERTISE

- Excellent strategic strengths with keen ability to develop operational plans and achieve organizational goals.
- Resourceful coordinator with experience in budget preparation and financial management.
- Well developed ability to conceptualize, research, organize and implement special projects.
- Good insight and ability to anticipate and identify problems as well as generate solutions in a complex work environment among diversified stakeholders.
- Diplomatic communicator encompassing keen political acumen for consulting, liaising and networking.
- Expertise in public relations/media including radio, television and print.
- Excellent human resource skills with experience in hiring, delegating responsibility and conducting evaluations.
- Superior empathy, interpersonal and communication skills with ability to foster individual growth and empower client contacts.
- Committed to learning, mastering new skills and knowledge.

ACCOMPLISHMENTS

- Established and managed office for non-profit corporation.
- Conceived and coordinated services and benefits for 400+ clients.
- Maintained complete financial records for non-profit corporation and own business.
- Facilitated workshops, at provincial and national level, on a variety of subjects related to small business and child care.
- Served as consultant/advisor to several national organizations and contributed to special national projects.
- Established and ran extremely successful child care business for seven years.

EMPLOYMENT HISTORY

Executive Director, Branville Housing Association, 1987 – April 1996
Administrative Assistant, Vice-President, Landways Slides, Toronto
Canadian Sales Manager, Rink Canada, Toronto

PROFESSIONAL DEVELOPMENT/EDUCATION

Workshops, seminars and conferences; marketing strategies; accreditation models; management styles; public relations; public policy; cross-cultural curriculum development; respecting cultural diversities; financial management and tax issues.

Word Perfect 5.0, St. Vital School Division, Continuing Education Division
Manitoba Child Care Worker II Classification, Red River Community College
Administrative Assistant Certificate, Secord Business College, Toronto

COMMUNITY AND PROFESSIONAL AFFILIATIONS

Winnipeg Chamber of Commerce
Winnipeg Newcomers Club – Chair
Boy Scouts of Canada – Division Leader

LINDA DUBUCINI

1795 – 70 Fort Street
Arnprior, Ontario
T1R 2P8

Res: (519) 957-7940

An accomplished personnel/administrative professional with over twelve (12) years extensive experience in public sector, manufacturing and service industries. Detail oriented with commitment to high standards. Seeking professional challenges and career opportunities to become a key contributor in a team-oriented environment.

PROFESSIONAL EXPERTISE

- Efficient personnel and administrative management skills specializing in recruitment, selection and placement of professional and non-professional employees to meet the company's and clients' manpower requirements at the lowest possible cost.
- Solid background and thorough experience in the formulation and implementation of personnel policies, psychological testing, performance evaluation, wage and salary administration and computerized payroll using IBM38 and Royal Bank system.
- Effective counsellor in handling confidential personal and work related situations or problems of employees, clients and applicants.
- Excellent people skills and in depth sensitivity to the needs of individuals at all levels with openness, directness and fairness.
- Proficiency in prioritizing workloads, up-to-date personnel data bank and complete detailed documentation of interview/counselling reports.
- Successful track record in determining, developing and delivering tailored to fit, in-house seminar packages.

ACCOMPLISHMENTS

- Key Management Committee member responsible for the sound business operations and profitability of the company which resulted in the expansion of having three (3) additional school branches in two years.
- Contributed to expanding company's customer base through strategic marketing as well as delivery of course offerings and in-house seminar packages to business and government offices.

- A part-owner of a training school for 4 years which provided skill training services to hotel personnel, domestic helpers and janitorial services prior to their overseas contract to Middle East and Hong Kong.
- Appointed as a psychologist to work in Saudi Arabia in charge of recruitment and personnel/administrative management in a multi-national company.

EMPLOYMENT HISTORY

PERSONNEL CONSULTANT/COUNSELLOR — Donna's Personnel Services, May 1990 – April 1993

PERSONNEL/PAYROLL MANAGER — Sports Club Pant/Canadian Menswear, Feb. 1989 – April 1990

PERSONNEL/ADMINISTRATIVE MANAGER — Danna's Collosol Career Centre, Jan. 1982 – Jan. 1989

ADMINISTRATIVE SPECIALIST, INDUSTRIAL PSYCHOLOGIST, GUIDANCE COUNSELLOR, ENGLISH TEACHER — 1974 – 1981

PROFESSIONAL DEVELOPMENT/EDUCATIONAL BACKGROUND

Business Management Forum — Federal Business Development Bank, July 19 – August 27, 1993

Career Assessment Instruments for Business Industries	1989
Labour – Management Co-operation for Industrial Peace & Harmony	1989
Time Management	1985
HRD in Focus/Bridging the Effort for Survival	1985
Alternative Management Style	1982
Personnel Management	1977
Master of Arts – Industrial Psychology	1974 – 1979
Bachelor of Science in Education (Guidance Counselling)	1969 – 1974

Comprehensive Resource Lists

Appendix A

■

Professional

Expertise

Statements

Comprehensive Resource Lists

APPENDIX A - PROFESSIONAL EXPERTISE STATEMENTS

The following section contains skill statements that you can choose to use for your own résumé. You can use the statements exactly as they are or make minor changes and make them your own. Note that the skills statements are listed alphabetically.

Statements can be found for:

Accounting/Financing

- Accuracy and consistency complemented by excellent skills for the completion of bookkeeping and accounting tasks, journal entries, coding invoices, compiling data, preparing financial summaries, posting and balancing.
- Bottom-line financial orientation with creative leadership in resource allocation enabling a balanced budget and ongoing monitoring for eight divisions comprised of 40 departments with 80 full-time and 36 part-time programs.
- Corporate level financial and economic analysis skills and experience in major acquisition, divestiture or capital expenditure decisions.
- Demonstrated bottom-line accomplishments through solid supervision and management of financial reporting and control functions in a multi-million dollar operating environment.
- Excellent auditing skills, both external and internal, for the examination of records to disclose areas of loss under tax legislation or company policy and procedure.
- Excellent treasury and banking expertise including negotiating and structuring corporate credit facilities, foreign exchange and interest rate risk management, cash flow management and related policy development.
- Highly skilled in the design, revision, implementation and maintenance of accounting reporting systems for management and shareholders in sophisticated computerized environments.
- Keen business acumen and expertise in strategic financial planning resulting in business development, growth in profitability, and sales and the overall financial success of an organization.
- Strong accounting skills with extensive experience in sourcing and implementing manual and computerized accounting systems to process monthly financial statements, general ledger, accounts receivable, accounts payable, payroll and year end financial statements.

Administrative Support

- Ability to adapt generic systems to meet specific company needs by compiling, planning and writing office material manuals for future use.
- Highly developed administration strengths for the establishment of effective policies and procedures for general office management.
- Mature with discretion and judgement in handling confidential information.

- Strong ability to focus on policies and procedures, and development and control in corporate administration, operational, finance, treasury, and human resources areas.
- Well-developed organization, planning and administration strengths for confidential, corporate level services in sensitive executive and ministerial work environments.
- Skilled in the development and preparation of confidential correspondence, reports and policy manuals.
- Detail-oriented, skilled and experienced in co-ordinating details, confirming schedules and deterring appointment conflicts.
- Efficient administrative and organizational abilities; skilled at word processing, management, assembly of monthly reports, and researching and making travel arrangements.
- Proficient in the operation of a busy switchboard and reception area, able to communicate with callers in a professional and customer service manner.

Analytical/Problem Solving

- Creative problem solving approach to meeting customer needs complemented by a keen ability to initiate, recommend and create strategic alliances with interested key stakeholders.
- Demonstrated analytical, innovative and creative problem solving and decision making capabilities coupled with effective trouble shooting skills developed through productivity analysis of measurable results.
- Excellent problem solving and conflict resolution skills for participatory staff involvement and issues management.
- Excellent analytical strengths for complex organizational analysis, productivity improvement, work simplification, job analysis and major systems design.
- Highly developed analytical skills supported by demonstrated strengths in financial management and computer business applications.
- Innovative problem solver; able to proactively develop efficient solutions to challenges in a variety of work environments.
- Keen problem solving strengths with an innovative, creative approach to resolving problems and challenges.
- People-oriented, humanistic approach to problem solving with keen ability to develop trust in an encouraging and supportive work and customer service environment.

- Solid foundation and significant expertise in the application of process improvement and total quality strategies in all areas of operations management in order to ensure the highest standards of customer service.
- Visionary strategic planner with keen ability to identify and assess the impact of changing environmental conditions on an organization, match resources to short and long term goals and set priorities.

Business Development/Business Planning

- Accomplished ability in business plan development and achievement of revenue and profit.
- A keen profit awareness not only for initiating client programs which protect company profits and produce volume but also by preparing and managing department budgets effectively with a constant examination of creative cost savings.
- Demonstrated ability to manage over 200 clients maintaining accurate record administration and ensuring prompt collection of accounts.
- Demonstrated bottom-line accomplishments attained through solid supervision and management of operations in a multi-million dollar operating climate.
- Entrepreneurial and inventive, with an attitude towards success, complemented by intense results-oriented drive.
- Exceptionally creative with substantial ability and success in the identification of customer and business trends, the identification and exploitation of market opportunities, conducting competitive analysis and the initiation and design of co-venture programming.
- Keen business development skills for evaluation, goal setting, start-up opportunities, acquisitions and joint ventures with successful bottom line performance.
- Proven resourcefulness and innovativeness in startup, day-to-day operations and damage control within the oil, mining, aerospace and hi-tech manufacturing sectors.
- Proven track record in developing existing business and identifying and pursuing opportunities.
- Solid business acumen with extensive experience and educational foundation in business start-up, management, promotion, marketing and sales.
- Top notch entrepreneurial skills for the effective planning, organization and administration of a regional based business.

- Well developed entrepreneurial perception with exceptional organizational and co-ordinating strengths for the start up of new business ventures, community based projects and special events.

Communications/Public Relations

- Assertive and effective communication skills; able to provide written and verbal summaries/briefings/reports that are easily understood and logically presented.
- Assertive and effective communication skills when interacting with the public, committees, board of directors, community organizations and government agencies.
- Effective communication skills for the establishment and development of strong working relationships with business, industry, education and government colleagues as well as staff at all levels.
- Effective communication skills for the establishment of strong working relationships with business professionals, banking officials and suppliers.
- Excellent communication and interpersonal skills for effective teamwork, staff management and the development of sound working relationships with suppliers, clients and customers.
- Experienced in the research, development, implementation and evaluation of communication strategies.
- Good communication and interpersonal skills complemented by strong organization and ability to work both autonomously and as a team player.
- Quietly assertive with excellent communication skills enabling a solid relationship with suppliers, bankers, lawyers and auditors.
- Significant oral communication and presentation skills for direct sales solicitation, sales presentations, and internal staff training and development.
- Well developed communication skills for effective customer/staff relations.
- Well developed research and interview expertise combined with strong presentation skills.
- Working knowledge of radio and television production as well as limited experience with on air responsibilities.

Community Development

- Able to analyze and prepare detailed feasibility studies and develop an implementation framework and action plan for community and economic development projects.
- Able to administer an economic development fund and conduct post loan counseling and project evaluation.
- Highly skilled in the directing and co-ordinating of input required for economic development projects from project description through to monitoring.
- Strong understanding of and ability to promote programs and services to targeted clientele.
- Superior level of expertise and knowledge of community resources and support networks for education, self-improvement and family assistance which enables effective service for children and families.
- Thorough understanding of program design, development, implementation and evaluation of new or existing initiatives.
- Solid working knowledge of community collaboration concepts for the development of action projects directed towards the improvement of quality of life.
- Highly skilled in the application of strategies and mechanisms to link ad hoc community initiatives and groups into established structures.
- Well developed community development toolkit, inclusive of techniques, discussion and decision making techniques, action planning tools, process review strategies, and evaluation tools.

Computer/Information Technology

- Able to install and upgrade server applications tools, allocate systems storage, plan for future storage requirements, create primary database storage structures, modify database structures and provide security services.
- Ability to plan and implement information technology strategies, and develop user teams for large scale technology transitions.
- Broad knowledge and experience in matching appropriate technologies, designs and systems development techniques with organizations needs, capabilities and resources.
- Computer literate in both mainframe and personal computing utilizing spreadsheets, word processing and automated office, including local and wide area networks.

- Documentation expertise in the areas of forms design, screen design, user guide development, application guides development, document cataloguing and management, workflow analysis and DIP experience.
- Excellent skills in software development including the design and implementation of new projects as well as the creation of enhancements and maintenance of exiting software products.
- Highly skilled in using a structured development methodology approach, data modelling, systems documentation and project management skills within a client server environment.
- Proficient in the initiation and programming of PC applications in a service-oriented environment resulting in improving response time as well as more accurate, up-to-date and detailed management information.
- Strong computer expertise for major computer program revisions, planning, research, trouble shooting, and consultation within an office environment.
- Strong knowledge of business software and hardware. Hands on understanding of selection, implementation and operation of systems to achieve cost effectiveness and strategic advantage.

Customer Service

- Expertise in customer service and the resolution of customer dissatisfaction.
- Good customer service orientation for working with a wide range of clientele including the disabled, senior population, children, private and public sectors.
- High degree of professional integrity with excellent public relations strengths resulting in the development of solid business relationships with customers and suppliers.
- Proven customer service focus complemented by administrative management strengths to build work systems that support consistently high service standards.
- Solid communication and interpersonal skills for good working relationships with customers; able to assist from identification of needs to completion of tasks.
- Solid foundation and team membership experience in developing a total quality management and innovative customer service corporate culture.
- Strong sense of customer service with experience in the field of service and sales.

- Superior customer service focus with keen ability to develop and exceed service excellence in a total quality service environment.

Counselling/Employee Assistance

- Able to act as peer to subordinates and peers on matters related to career advancement, abuse, harassment and other personal matters that may have impact on an employee's job performance.
- Cool head in a time of crisis with expertise in the prevention of suicide.
- Empathetic listener with intuitive strengths and rapid decision making ability.
- Strong assessment skills for the identification of client's physical, emotional and spiritual need prior to placement of appropriate personnel.
- Superior empathy, interpersonal and communication skills with ability to foster personal growth and empower client contacts.
- Well developed interviewing, counseling and analytical skills; able to quickly understand and identify client needs and issues; establish safety and security and facilitate effective problem resolution.
- Holistic counseling and conceptual framework, skilled at identifying client needs and systematically integrating selected methods and approaches to facilitate client behavior change.
- Highly skilled in the application of cognitive learning and restructuring approach able to challenge self-defeating client beliefs and attitudes and assist clients to mobilize resources toward building personal independence.
- Well developed socio-emotional skills; able to respond spontaneously and effectively to a wide range of client needs, able to assist clients in both one-on-one and group intervention strategies.

Government/Regulated Environments

- Experienced in the participation of government advisory committees and coalitions in the areas of government restructuring, race relations, diversity, discrimination, and equality and community development.
- Highly developed political savvy and judgement skills for working with elected officials, boards, agencies and the public, complemented by extensive experience in negotiating multi level collaborations and strategic partnerships.
- Highly skilled in consultation and collaboration with government and community agencies to spearhead, design and develop policies and programs to promote multiracial harmony.

- Highly skilled in the leadership of task forces and committee structures which require collaboration with unions and community stakeholders to design, develop and strategize the application of new and broad ranging policies and programs.
- In-depth working knowledge of board-managed associations, combined with good group facilitation skills for project management and community leadership.
- Keen understanding of and practical management experience in a highly regulated environment with a working knowledge of municipal and provincial legislation regarding mineral claims, land rights, general leases, railroad leases, as well as health, safety and environmental regulations.
- Keen understanding of municipal and provincial government functions with the ability to write, present, defend proposals, and work collaboratively in sensitive and dynamic relationships.
- Significant expertise and experience in the proactive development of policy initiatives in the areas of culture and race relations within municipal, provincial, national and international environments.
- Well developed understanding of government structure and processes with ability to lead, manage and chair various committees and task forces which provide for public participation into facilitating legislative change.

Hospitality

- Detail oriented with well developed skills in the analysis of administrative, financial and inventory systems, policies and procedures. Proven strengths in the design, development and implementation of organizational structures to support retail and hospitality environments.
- Excellent co-ordination and organizational skills with successful accomplishments in large, high profile culinary events, professional and political conferences.
- Good understanding and ability to monitor market trends, create and develop new catering menus, catering manuals and develop and deliver customer service training programs.
- Proven ability to manage complex events and projects to successful completion in large facilities of up to 35,000 square feet of conference meeting space.
- Proven strengths in financial management including budgets, cost based analysis, point of sale and inventory control systems and marketing plans within the hospitality industry.

- Public relations strengths and interpersonal skills for effective development of business and working relationships with customers and suppliers.
- Solid foundation in hospitality systems with keen ability to identify problems and increase productivity and profitability through staff recruitment, selection, training and continuous improvement programs.
- Solid organizational skills for the successful operation of a 200 seat, full service restaurant with consistently high achievement ratings for service, cleanliness, procedural integrity and guest service as determined by a corporate testing division.
- Superior customer service focus with keen ability to develop and exceed service excellence in food and beverage operation for hotel/resort environments.
- Well developed abilities to lead and participate in the design and development of multi-million dollar expansions of guest rooms, food and beverage facilities including equipment procurement.

Human Resources (Personnel)

- Accomplished human resource management strengths including compensation, staffing, interviewing, performance reviews, job descriptions and evaluations, conflict resolution, training and teambuilding.
- Demonstrated ability to integrate human resources with other corporate business plans to attain productivity improvements and cost reductions.
- Excellent interpersonal and human resource management strengths with capacity to work with a variety of people in a dynamic, supportive and participative work environment.
- Expert knowledge of benefit designs, contacts, underwriting, pricing, administration, claims control and accounting.
- Proficient in utilizing innovative ways to recruit, motivate and develop a work team environment within a non-profit environment.
- Solid expertise in the design and development of human resource compensation and benefit systems including flexible benefits, cost containment, early retirement and pension planning.
- Solid human resources management skills including planning, recruitment, selection, supervision, employee relations, salary and benefits administration, contract negotiations, training and development, personnel policy development, job descriptions, performance appraisal and job evaluation.

- Solid human resource, team leadership and interpersonal strengths for the motivation and management of professional, technical and administrative staff components.
- Solid understanding of employee benefit programs with specific skills in the research, planning, analysis and negotiation of the most cost effective plans.
- Solid working knowledge of current legislation regarding labour standards, fair employment practices, collective agreements, health and safety and unemployment insurance with ability to undertake responsibility to ensure company compliance.

Interpersonal Skills

- Effective interpersonal skills motivation and in multi-disciplinary and team environments for efficient utilization of all resources.
- Excellent interpersonal skills resulting in above standard staff performance and relationships and reduced absenteeism.
- Excellent interpersonal skills resulting in the establishment of terrific working relationships with all internal, external and government advisors.
- Excellent interpersonal communication strengths with a flair for group dynamics and the development of solid relationships and networks.
- Good interpersonal and leadership skills facilitating a positive team-oriented management style in both corporate and regional work environments.
- Solid interpersonal skills with demonstrated ability to direct individuals in a team concept environment which includes fellow workers, clients and the general public.
- Skilled motivator of a team focused upon successful achievement of objectives.
- Superior interpersonal skills for the interpretation of corporate and employee needs, allowing for the provision of relevant, timely and accurate information dissemination.
- Well developed interpersonal skills ensuring effective dealings at all levels of an organization.

Leadership

- Effective leadership and team building strengths; able to analyze requirements, identify skills and motivate a team to successfully complete projects.

- Effective supervisory strengths for the management of a multi-unit organization with varied levels of professional and administrative personnel.
- Effective task orientation with expertise in delegating responsibility, ensuring harmony, establishing work priorities and schedules, dealing with concerns of clients and staff, conducting reviews and evaluations of systems and programs.
- Management team leadership strengths with specific expertise in delegation of responsibility, establishing commitment, setting work priorities and schedules, addressing concerns of customers and staff members.
- Natural leadership strengths with strong communication and interpersonal skills for effective development of sound teamwork relationships.
- Participative team management style with a strong focus on identification of staff roles and responsibilities; articulation of clear, concise and accurate expectations; and the provision of employee development.
- Practical, hands-on approach to problems with solid technical ability to manage small financial and construction problems.
- Proactive team leadership skills; capable of innovative and practical problem resolution in the financial, administrative and staff development areas.
- Quiet, mentor/leader management style with ability and experience in supervision of technical personnel in a laboratory and machine shop environment.
- Strong leadership, communication and consulting skills for executive management directorship and committee chair in the private sector, not-for-profit sector, and service organizations.

Negotiation

- Conciliatory expertise utilized in developing and maintaining satisfactory relationships within a unionized environment.
- Creative expertise in negotiations preparation, strategy and tactics.
- Effective and persuasive negotiation strengths with a deep appreciation of the quality and value of a diverse group of people holding wide ranging views.
- Effective and persuasive strengths with demonstrated use of the win/win processes to gain consensus and understanding.

- High level of expertise in complex negotiations for union/work agreements, compliance to regulatory control legislation and land lease agreements.
- Keen intuition and the ability to counsel, negotiate and resolve conflict.
- Negotiation strengths with ability to negotiate contracts with vendors, external clients.
- Proven investigative and negotiation skills ensuring effective and appropriate intervention.
- Solid working knowledge of contract negotiations and capital acquisition with ability to review and input to a variety of contracts and legal documents.
- Strengths in the negotiation of agreements within a customer driven environment.
- Strong belief in win/win negotiation processes for agreement and understanding.

Conflict Management

- Strong understanding of conflicts as an organizational process; skilled and experienced in the design of policies and processes that constructively draw conflict to the forefront and provide opportunities to resolve issues effectively.
- Holistic approach to effective conflict management, exceptional understanding of organizational dynamics; supportive of participatory processes to developing high quality dispute resolution.
- Well-developed systems thinking approach to organizational changes and conflict management; able to assess interrelated areas of dysfunction and develop collaborative strategies for intervention.
- Experienced in participating in a corporate alternative dispute process; trained in joint problem solving methods, able to act as a neutral advisor.
- Well developed understanding of the methods principles and stages of systems design for conflict resolution; experienced in facilitating group conflict sessions.
- Confident in personal conflict resolution skills, keen sensitivity and strengths in the identification of specific issues, able to clarify and prioritize issues for resolution.

Non-profit Management

- Experience in not-for-profit organizations including the incorporation, establishment of policies and procedures, recruitment of volunteers and fundraising.
- Highly skilled in the recruitment, training and co-ordinating of volunteers, developing volunteer recognition programs.
- Significant expertise and experience in the role of Executive Director, with strengths in administrative operations, supervision of staff, preparation and presentation of financial reports, program and policy development, implementation and administration.
- Significant strengths in board management at the local, provincial and national levels.
- Skilled program development specialist with ability to initiate, design, develop, implement and evaluate both small and large scale programs.
- Well developed skills in working effectively with volunteer boards and committees to prepare intermediate operational and business plans.

Operations Management

- Able to manage all responsibilities of print shop operation including tendering, quotes, stock ordering, artwork delegation, printing job, collating, cutting, folding and final packaging, account preparation, postage metering, mail handling, inventory and stock control as well as budget preparation.
- Ability to initiate and manage office administration including receivable and payable accounts, correspondence and record keeping.
- Accomplished at developing management systems and effecting change through skill development and coaching.
- Competent administrative skills with ability to undertake budgeting, analyze variance and profitability reports.
- Consistent and successful record of managing financial budget and operational resources in a wide range of administrative positions.
- Detail-oriented with well developed skills in analysis of administrative, financial, and inventory systems, policies and procedures.
- Proven strengths in the design, development and implementation of organizational structures to support corporate environment.
- Executive level management and team leadership skills for tackling the full range of executive concerns and issues.
- Excellent operational and administrative expertise for the functional management of a corporate branch office.

- Excellent strategic strengths with keen ability to develop operational plans to meet organizational goals.
- Extensive, in-depth, executive management skills and experience in large, multi-service, multi-product, retail sales environments including travel and entertainment.
- Extensive experience and expertise in strategic and operational planning with skills in the management of planning within a large and complex work environment.

Organizational Skills

- Adept at managing details with ability to plan, schedule, analyze needs and develop priorities in order to carry out responsibilities in an independent manner.
- Excellent organizational abilities with extensive experience in the public sector, municipal committee leadership as well as small business start-up and management.
- Excellent organizational and administrative ability with superior strengths in planning and attention to detail.
- Excellent organizational and planning strengths for large facility and events management including policy development and implementation, formulation and implementation of business plan.
- Excellent organizational skills for the accomplishment of tasks within a specific timeframe.
- Excellent organizational skills for delivery and prioritizing service to client sensitive environment.
- Excellent organizational skills with ability to manage a large residential facility including staff supervisors and maintenance and customer relations.
- Good organization and planning skills for policy development, formulation and implementation of a formal business plan, including forecasting, budgeting, and attention to the bottom line.
- Organizational strengths for planning, scheduling, implementing and follow-up of varied, multi-scoped projects.
- Proven ability to organize single and multi-unit operations resulting in increased sales and customer satisfaction.
- Skilled in managing details with ability to plan and schedule, analyze needs and priorities and carry out responsibilities in an independent manner.

Policy Development/Analysis

- Able to supply meaningful input for the development of corporate policy.
- Proficient in the communication of results to members, customers and company personnel.
- Extensive experience in policy analysis and development in formulating corporate/department goals and in providing leadership to achieve target results.
- Highly skilled and extensive experience in the development and implementation of operational policy manuals which include job descriptions, employee orientation and performance evaluation programs.
- Skilled in the creation of policy, procedure and administrative manuals. Able to maintain over significant numbers of confidential client records.
- Skilled in the interpretation of the impact of local and national policies.
- Skilled in the systematic collection, analysis and presentation of data for the evaluation of programs and policy effectiveness.
- Well-developed field work techniques for policy and program review, strengths in research design, sampling procedures and measuring outcomes.
- Skilled in the conduct of operational reviews for evaluation of program compliance and policy implementation.
- Experienced in program review and evaluation in the areas of education, social welfare, health, housing, mental health, legal services and economic development.
- Solid working knowledge of and experience in effective planning and policy analysis; skilled at researching contingencies and alternatives for policy implementation.

Project Management

- Action-oriented, innovative, able to meet time and budget targets by strategic planning while employing logic and ingenuity.
- Excellent abilities to follow instructions and to complete responsibilities within assigned deadlines.
- Extensive experience in initiating and co-ordinating complex corporate projects.

- Excellent project management strengths for successful and timely completion of complex work programs within contract framework.
- Excellent strategic organizational planning and co-ordination skills for project and program initiation, staffing, start up, implementation and timely completion within limited budgets and resources.
- Good project management skills with ability to cost estimate, identify and allocate resources, and follow work through to completion and provide appropriate evaluations.
- Significant working knowledge of business process re-design with experience in arranging cost control inventory systems to limit stationary retention.
- Solid project management skills complemented by high quality work standards enabling the completion of work within difficult time frames.
- Strong organizational skills for developing and implementing complex projects with a keen awareness for deadlines.
- Superior project management skills with significant expertise in the management of diverse projects including identification of issues, planning, implementation, and monitoring for successful completion.

Research

- Able to conduct data collection for acceptance test reports, component failure analysis and trend analysis; able to test and troubleshoot computers, printed circuit boards, power supplies, cables and components.
- Excellent investigative skills and ability to develop conceptual frames and theories using the principles of irreversible thermodynamics.
- Highly sophisticated strengths in atomic physics, fundamental quantum theories, applied mathematics, non-linear analysis and physical chemistry.
- Significant laboratory skills for the preparation, organization, and co-ordination of test experiments involving interdisciplinary teams of physicists, chemists and engineers.
- Significant numerical methods research strengths for studies in radiative transfer in the atmosphere, gas ignition and biomass systems, and fluid flow.
- Significant research skills for assessment, feasibility studies, preliminary design, and evaluation studies within the environmental engineering studies field.

- Solid working knowledge of scientific investigation of biophysical and biochemical processes using the principles of irreversible thermodynamics.
- Strengths in managing a multi-disciplinary scientific and technological research project, complemented by extensive experience in negotiating multi-partner collaborations.
- Well developed ability to conceptualize, research, organize and implement specific projects.
- Well developed research and writing skills with experience in writing and editing a weekly economic analysis report outlining the agricultural conditions in the province.
- Well developed research and writing skills complemented by the ability to translate scientific technical documents between English, French and German.

Sales And Marketing

- Accomplished at creating marketable and profitable products and services.
- Dynamic, creative sales and marketing techniques enabling the attainment of corporate team objectives.
- Exemplary knowledge and application of the psychological principles of selling, complemented by very strong interpersonal skills which confirms abilities as a team leader, trainer and coach.
- Extensive and diverse experience gained through effective experience within the major retail trades ranging from the sales floor to the board room to successfully implement corporate selling plans.
- Highly skilled in idea generation and promotional planning. Able to create and implement plans including special events, direct sales, sales incentive programs, price lists/catalogues and shows to achieve and exceed sales objectives.
- Highly skilled in promotional planning and design including special events, sales promotion packages and annual marketing plans utilizing a variety of mass media.
- Skilled in strategic planning for corporate marketing and sales programming complemented by a strong personal customer service and customer satisfaction philosophy.
- Strong ability to be a calculating risk taker who implements creative practical solutions for achieving both company and clients success resulting in mutual satisfaction and long term relationships.

- Superior skills in the initiation, management and growth with strong emphasis on enhanced corporate image and client relationship building.
- Superior strategic planning strengths in sales and marketing with the unique ability to conceive, design and implement internal and external corporate programs.

Strategic Planning

- Ability to initiate, develop and implement short and long term strategies and their associated tactics.
- Able to participate as a key member of the management team to provide the backup and technical assistance to develop a strategic plan ensuring the growth of an organization.
- Action-oriented innovator able to meet time and budget by strategic planning while employing logic and ingenuity.
- Effective strategic planning strengths with the ability to create a long-term focus and to communicate this information to all levels of the organization resulting in business development and growth in profitability.
- Excellent strategic strengths with keen ability to develop operational plans to meet organization goals.
- Strategic planning insight complemented by rigorous analytical capability developed through experience with a variety of companies in different situations and industries.
- Substantial skills in strategic planning for the development of long-term corporate plans complemented by ability to focus activities toward the goal.
- Well-developed strategic planning skills to analyze and determine the short term and long term organizational directions.
- Keen sensitivity to organizational dynamics and the impact on strategy implementation; skilled at developing accommodating processes to facilitate internal support for new initiatives.
- Solid understanding of the political strategy and techniques for the development of aggressive competitive strategic action plans; skilled at leading the assessment of business trends, threats and opportunities, internal and external political capabilities and the negotiation of alliance opportunities.

Teamwork

- Ability to gain the confidence and support of employees in respect to integrity and fair play.

- Ability to work both as a team player and autonomously complemented by good communication and interpersonal skills.
- Able to work equally well as a team player or independently.
- Detailed and results driven with participative management style emphasizing individual growth, active involvement and increased team morale.
- Excellent interpersonal and human resource management strengths with capacity to work with a variety of people in a dynamic, supportive and participative work environment.
- Self-directed, energetic team leadership strengths with a preference for undertaking significant responsibility.
- Solid foundation and team membership experience in developing a total quality management and innovative customer service corporate culture.
- Solid knowledge of group dynamics with keen sensitivity to team members and an ability to form, direct and lead multi-disciplinary professionals.
- Strong organizational strengths for the supervision, co-ordination and implementation of management work plans, process improvement initiatives and staffing in a fast paced production environment.
- Team-oriented individual with good interpersonal skills for good customer and staff relations.
- Well developed communication and interpersonal skills for effective teamwork and customer/staff relations.

Technical/Manufacturing/Engineering

- Comprehensive strengths and experience in the fabrication of precision aerospace components, research instruments, health care and other complex equipment.
- Demonstrated ability to provide insight into efficiency production resulting in cost savings and more efficient utilization of human resources.
- Exceptional skills and innate ability in the field of mechanical design complemented by over 40 years of creative and practical experience in a research, clinical and prototype environment.
- Good technical skills for the maintenance of small machines such as photocopiers, cameras, VCR's and drill press.
- Highly developed technical knowledge of manufacturing processes, control systems and engineering projects.

- Proven resourcefulness and innovativeness in the start-up, day-to-day operations and damage control for the oil, mining, aerospace and hi-tech manufacturing sectors.
- Solid foundation and working knowledge of machining, manufacturing processes, drafting, CAD drafting, joining technology, welding, surface finishing, mechanical actuators and mechanisms, electro mechanical devices, motor and gear drives, hydraulics, air controls, photography and carpentry.
- Solid maintenance and property management skills for effective facility upkeep, security provisions and equipment control.
- Well developed skill in the utilization of many metals and common plastics particularly as employed in medical applications.

Total Quality Management/Quality Assurance Business Process Re-design

- Able to lead, guide and train quality inspection work force teams to promote and maintain an acceptable level in quality at the least cost.
- Able to use quality expertise to provide technical assistance to manufacturing departments, investigate and provide feedback on quality problems.
- Advanced quality management expertise including statistical process control, gage record and calibration systems and failure mode and effect analysis.
- Excellent ability to develop quality manual documentation which meets quality audit inspection and national standards.
- Outstanding and thorough application of problem solving and trouble shooting techniques with exceptional enthusiasm towards continuous quality improvements.
- Significant working knowledge of business process re-design with experience in arranging cost control inventory systems to limit stationary retention.
- Skilled in the investigation and feedback of information on quality problems; able to analyze data, initiate corrective action reports and lead meetings to deal with non conformance.
- Skills and experience in the writing and updating of Quality Assurance Operating Procedures, test procedures and manufacturing processes and the development of manuals and instructional tools.
- Skilled quality auditor for FordQ101, including special expertise in failure mode and effect analysis, advance quality planning, statistical process control, gage record and calibrations systems.

- Well developed skills and experience in the conduct of quality planning improvements, process capability studies, document preparation and supervision of quality improvement projects.
- Well developed training methodologies for the guidance and training of inspection work teams to promote and maintain acceptable levels of quality for the least cost.

Training and Development/Group Facilitation

- Able to facilitate group discussions and planning meetings in order to develop consensus decision making between the varied interests of multiple stakeholders.
- Comprehensive training expertise complemented by extensive people skills, able to provide guidance and leadership resulting in significant employee contributions.
- Demonstrated workshop design, development and delivery strengths with ability to apply skills in a wide range of interesting and challenging environments.
- Highly skilled in the design, development and delivery of presentations in the classroom and on the job.
- Proven training and development consulting skills with specific strengths in board development, problem solving and staff training.
- Skilled in the preparation of training manuals based on government legislation, policies and practices with consideration for the cultural milieu in which the training is taking place.
- Solid foundation in adult training and development skills, expertise and experience in technical training, organizational change and assertiveness leadership.
- Solid success and over six years' experience with disabled client rehabilitation; e.g. job teaching, monitoring progress, evaluating performance and conference reporting.
- Specialized skills in the development of training programs including product knowledge, communications and research.
- Strong foundation in adult learning principles with extensive experience in the design and delivery of staff development programs.
- Strong training skills with proven experience in working with people of all cultures and backgrounds.

Workplace Health and Safety

- Good training skills for the development and delivery of regional training programs in the transportation of dangerous goods WHMIS and quality customer service.
- Keen political acumen with expertise in the impact assessment of policy, procedures and regulations on health care in particular in the nursing profession.
- Solid knowledge of cleanliness health standards for working in a public working environment.
- Solid understanding of workplace health and safety standards and ability to maintain quality control and represent department issues on Workplace Health & Safety Committee.
- Solid understanding of workplace health and safety requirements; able to provide consultation to managers and training to staff and team leaders.

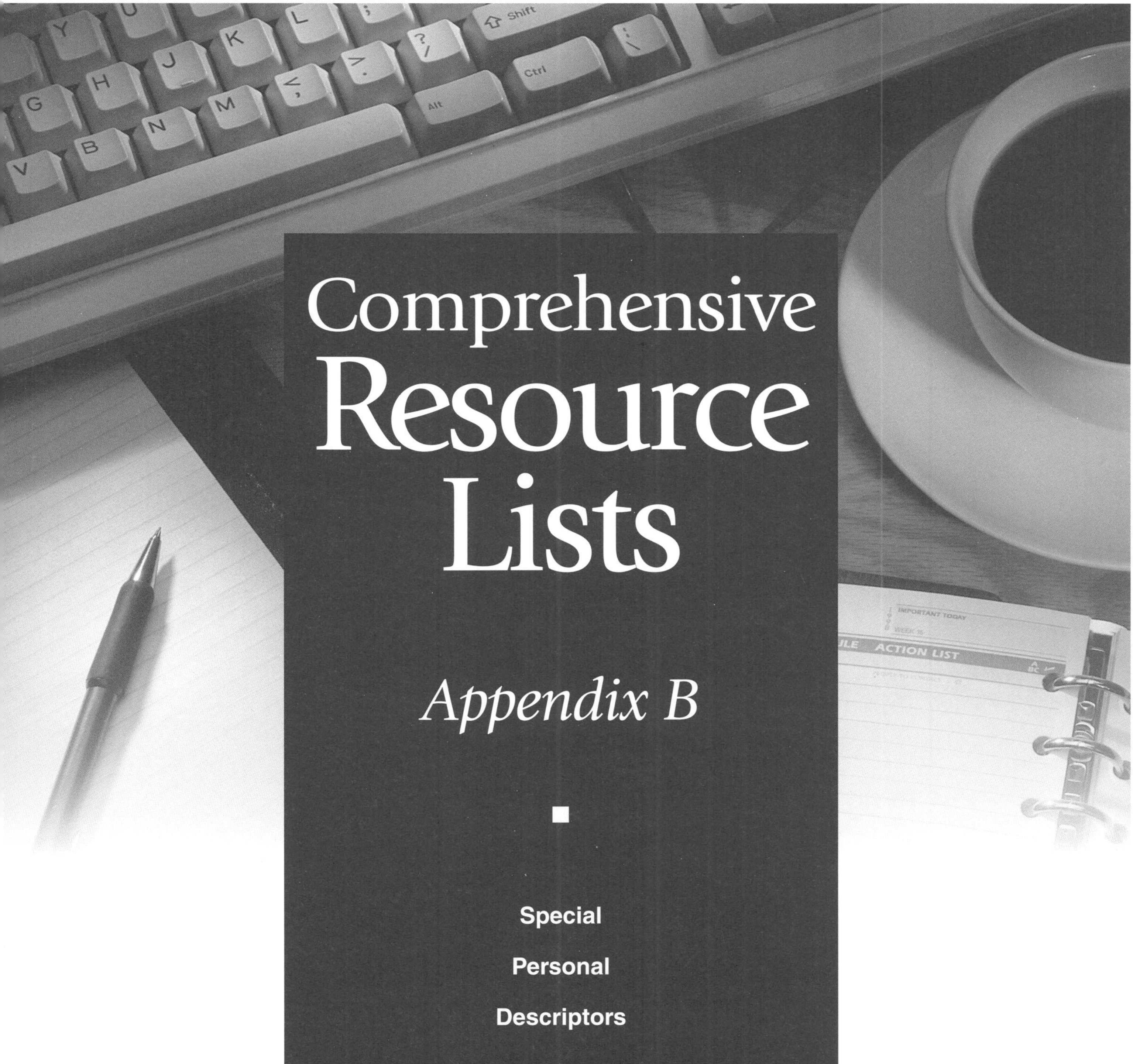

Comprehensive Resource Lists

Appendix B

■

Special

Personal

Descriptors

APPENDIX B - SPECIAL PERSONAL DESCRIPTORS

The following section contains special words, descriptors and phrases that will help you to write your summary personal profile. They include personal traits and ability phrases, as well as, leadership style, work environment and career objective statements that you can incorporate into your personal profile summary.

Select any words or phrases that best match who you are. You can then exchange these phrases for others within the summary profile or you can turn directly to page 75 and select a complete profile summary that best matches your personal situation.

Personal Trait Words

A

Above average	Achievement	Admired
Abstract	Achiever	Adroit
Academic-oriented	Acknowledged	Advanced
Accepting	Active	Advocate
Acclaimed	Active-oriented	Agent
Accommodating	Adamant	All around
Accomplished	Adaptable	All-American
Accountable	Adequate	All-Canadian

B

Backbone	Big hearted	Bright
Balanced	Bilingual	Broad minded
Basic	Blue chip	Broad shouldered
Bastion	Blue ribbon	Buffer
Beginner	Boaster	Bureaucratic
Beneficent	Bold	Business focus
Best	Bonded	Business like
Biased	Bottom line	

C

Calculating
Calm
Candid
Capable
Captivating
Card carrying
Career-minded
Careful
Caring
Carrier
Casual
Catalyst
Catalytic
Cautious
Celebrated
Celebrity
Certain
Certified
Challenged
Changeable
Charismatic
Charitable
Circumspect
Citified
Civic-minded
Civil
Clairvoyant
Classic
Clear
Clear thinking
Clear-headed
Clear-sighted
Clever
Close-mouthed
Co-anchor
Co-editor
Co-operative
Coherent
Cohesive
Collaborative
Collegial
Commanding
Commercial
Committed
Communicative
Community-oriented
Compassionate
Compatible
Compelling
Composed
Conceptual
Concerned
Conciliative
Concise
Concrete
Confident
Confident
Conforming
Conservative
Considerate
Consistent
Constructive
Contributor
Cordially
Corporate
Cosmopolitan
Cost-conscious
Courageous
Courteous
Creative
Credible
Curious

D

Daring
Decision-maker
Decisive
Dedicated
Deliberate
Delicate
Demanding
Dependable
Detail-oriented
Determined
Diagnostic
Diamond in the rough
Different
Diligent
Diminutive
Diplomatic
Direct
Disciplined
Discreet
Discriminating
Distinctive
Distinguished
Diverse
Down to Earth
Dramatic
Dreamer
Driven
Dynamic

E

Eager
Early
Earnest
Earthy
Easy going
Eclectic
Economical
Educated
Effective
Efficient
Eloquent
Empathetic
Energetic
Energized
Enlightened
Enterprising
Enthusiastic
Entrepreneurial
Established
Ethical
Exacting
Excel
Exceptional
Excited
Experienced
Expert
Expressive

F

Fair-minded
Faithful
Fantastic
Far sighted
Fast talker
Fast-thinking
Fearless
Firm
Flexible
Focused
Forceful
Forthright
Forward
Frank
Freelance
Friendly
Frugal
Fun
Futuristic

G

Gallant
Generalist
Generator
Generous
Genial
Gentle
Genuine
Glamorous
Globalist
Globe trotter
Goal-oriented
Good judgement
Good listener
Graceful
Gracious
Graduate
Graphic
Grassroots
Gregarious
Groomed
Ground crew
Grounded
Group-oriented
Growth potential
Growth-oriented
Guarded
Guide past

H

Habitual
Hands-on
Handy
Happy
Hard core
Hard line
Hard nosed
Hard working
Hardy
Harmonious
Head hunter
Headmaster
Healthy
Hearty
Heroic
Heuristic
High achiever
High energy
High fashion
High flying
High minded
High profile
High spirited
Historical
Holistic
Honest
Honorable
Honored
Hopeful
Humanistic
Humble
Humorous

I

Icon
Idea person
Idealist
Idealistic
Illuminated
Imaginative
Immune
Impact player
Impassioned
Impeccable
Impetuous
Important
Impressive
In-depth
Incredible
Independent
Individualistic
Infectious
Influential
Informal
Informative
Informed
Ingrained
Inhibited
Initiative
Innocent
Insatiable
Insightful
Insincere
Insistent
Inspiring
Instinctive
Instructive
Instrumental
Integrity
Intellectual
Intense
Interconnected
Interesting
Intermediate
International
Introspective
Intuitive
Inventive
Investigative
Issue-oriented

J

Joiner
Joker
Jovial
Judgmental
Judicious
Juggler
Juvenile

K

Keen
Keyman
Kind
Kindred spirit
Kingpin
Knowledgeable
Known

L

Laborious
Lady
Laid back
Leader
Leading edge
Learned
Legal
Legalistic
Legendary
Lenient
Level headed
Liberal-minded
Life saver
Lifeline
Light handed
Light hearted
Light-footed
Lightning rod
Lightweight
Like-minded
Likeable
Limited partner
Linear
Lineman
Linesman
Literal
Logical
Lone Ranger
Lookalike
Low key

M

Magnetic
Majestic
Manipulation
Marathoners
Marginal
Marketable
Marshmallow
Mannered
Martyr
Marvelous
Mascot
Massive
Master
Masterful
Masterwork
Matchmaker
Materialistic
Mathematical
Mature
Maverick
Maximize
Measured
Mechanistic
Meditative
Mellow
Melodramatic
Memorable
Mercenary
Merchandiser
Meritorious
Messenger
Methodical
Meticulous
Middle ground
Middle management
Middle weight
Midstream
Militant
Millwright
Mindful
Mindset
Ministerial
Mischievous
Mitigate
Mobility
Model
Moderate
Modern
Modest
Monolith
Mother hen
Motherly
Motivated
Multi-faceted
Multi-processing
Multifarious
Multilingual
Muscular
Musical
Mutually exclusive
Mysterious
Mythical

N

Narrator
Narrow
Narrow-minded
Nationalistic
Native
Natural
Naturalistic
Neat
Negative
Neighborly
Networked
Neutral
New
Newsworthy
Nice
Nighthawk
Nimble
Noble
Nominal
Non-judgmental
Nonchalant
Nonconformist
Nonpartisan
Numerical
Nurturing

O

Obedient
Objective
Obscurely
Observant
Officious
Old
Old guard
Old hand
Ombudsman
Onlooker
Open
Open-ended
Open-minded
Operationalistic
Opportunistic
Optimistic
Orderly
Organized
Original
Outgoing
Outspoken
Outstanding

P

Paced
Pacifier
Paradoxical
Parallel
Parochial
Partnership
Party-liner
Passionate
Paternalistic
Patient
Patriarch
Patriotic
Patron
Pawnbroker
Paymaster
Peacemaker
Pensive
People-oriented
Perceptive
Perfect
Perfectionist
Performer
Permanent
Permission
Persistent
Persona
Persuasive
Philosophical
Physical
Picture
Pioneer
Plain
Plateau
Platformer
Player
Playful
Pleasant
Pluralistic
Poised
Policy-making
Polished
Polite
Political
Politically aware
Popular
Positive
Potential
Powerbroker
Practical
Practitioner
Pragmatic
Precious
Precise

Preeminent
Preferential
Prejudicial
Premier
Premonition
Preoccupation
Prepared
Prestigious
Prime
Primitive
Princely
Principle
Principled
Private
Privileged
Pro-active
Problem-solver
Productive
Professional
Proficient
Profound
Programmer
Progressive
Project-oriented
Prolific
Prominent
Promising
Promoter
Prompt
Pronounced
Proper
Prophetic
Propriety
Prosperous
Protective
Protégé
Proud
Proven
Prowess
Prudent
Psychoanalytical
Punctual
Pure
Puritan
Purposeful
Puzzle
Pyramidal

Q

Quaint
Qualified
Quality
Quantum leap
Quarterback
Quick-learner
Quick-minded
Quiet
Quizzical

R

Race tracker
Racehorse
Racer
Radiant
Rag doll
Ragamuffin
Ragged
Rah-rah
Rain maker
Ramble
Range
Rare
Rarity
Rational
Ravenous
Ravishing
Raw material
Razzle dazzle
Reachable
Reactive
Read between the lines
Ready
Real
Realist
Realistic
Rearguard
Reasonable
Reasoned
Rebel
Rebound
Recharged
Recipient
Recognized
Recruit
Red ribbon
Referee
Refined
Reflective
Refreshing
Regal
Regards
Regimented
Regionalist
Regular
Rehearsing
Reinsuring
Relational
Relaxed
Relevant
Reliable

Religious
Reluctant
Remarkable
Reminiscent
Representative
Reputation
Resemblance
Reserved
Resident
Resilient
Resolute
Resourceful
Respectful
Responsible
Responsive
Restive
Restrained
Results-driven
Results-oriented
Retiring
Retreat
Right-minded
Rigid
Risk taker
Robust
Rough
Rough and ready
Rough around the edges
Rough neck
Royal
Rugged
Running mate
Rustic
Rusty

S

Sacred
Sacrifice
Safety
Safetyman
Sailor
Saleswoman/man/people
Sample
Sampler
Sanctimony
Sanctuary
Sappy
Savior
Scapegoat
Schemer
Schmoozer
Scholar
Schoolmaster
Scorekeeper
Scout
Scrupulous
Seasoned
Secondary
Secure
Security-oriented
Selective
Self-reliant
Self-assured
Self-controlled
Self-motivated
Self-starter
Sensitive
Serious
Service minded
Shrewd
Sincere
Skilled
Sociable
Solid
Sophisticated
Sound
Spontaneous
Stamina
Steady
Straight
Strategic
Strong
Substantial
Successful
Succinct
Superior
Supportive
Systematic

T

Table talk
Tact
Tactful
Tactical
Tactile
Talebearer
Talented
Taleteller
Talkative
Talker
Task-oriented
Teacher
Team player
Teammate
Technical
Technician
Technocrat
Technological
Telegraphic
Temperate
Tempered

Tenacious
Tendentious
Tenderfoot
Tenderhearted
Tentative
Tenured
Territorial
Thankful
Theatrical
Theoretical
Thinker
Thorough
Thoughtful
Thrifty
Tiger
Tight
Tight lipped
Timekeeper
Timespan
Toastmaster
Tolerant
Top achiever
Top flight
Tough
Tough minded
Towering
Tradition
Transact
Transcriber
Transient
Translucent
Transparent
Traveler
Tremendous
Trilingual
True
Trusting
Trustworthy
Tutorial
Two-dimensional

U

Ulterior
Ultimate
Ultra-careful
Ultra-cautious
Ultra-commercial
Utlra-critical
Ultra-energetic
Ultra-fashionable
Ultra-liberal
Ultra-powerful
Ultra-rational
Ultra-realistic
Ultra-sensitive
Unaffected
Unafraid
Unaided
Unassuming
Unbiased
Uncanny
Understanding
Understudy
Unfailing
Unique
Unpretentious
Unselfish
Unshakable
Unswerving
Upright
Upwardly mobile

V

Valiant
Valorous
Value added
Valued
Vanguard
Vehement
Vehicle
Vendor
Venerable
Venturesome
Verbalize
Verbose
Versatile
Vibrant
Vigorous
Visionary
Vitality
Vivacious
Vocal
Vociferous
Volunteer
Voracious
Votive
Vulnerable

W

Wallflower
War-horse
Warm
Warm-hearted
Warrior
Watchdog
Watchful
Watchman
Watchmen
Wealthy
Weighty
Well bided
Well-conditioned
Well-groomed
Well-grounded
Well-informed
Well-intentioned
Well-mannered
Well-meaning
Well-ordered
Well-rounded
Well-spoken
Wheeler dealer
Whimsical
Whirlwind
Who's who
Wholesome
Wide ranging
Wild cat
Wise
Witty
Wonderful
Workaholic
Workhorse
Workman
World class
World view
Worldly
Worldly minded
Worthy

Y

Yachtsman
Yardman
Yeoman

Z

Zest
Zesty

Personal Traits/Phrases

Look over the personal traits/phrases and select some that will fit your situation. Use them in your résumé summary or keep a list handy for when you want to describe a similar trait but in a different way.

- a well established and dynamic senior manager
- a leader in the field of
- a strategic thinker
- a keen understanding of the role of...
- a top achiever
- a passion for...
- a real contributor who wants to make a mark on an organization
- above average leadership and communication skills, self-motivated and competitive

- adept at working in a quality driven, team-oriented setting
- aggressive commitment to positive change
- an astute professional
- an effective delegator and motivator
- assertive self-starter
- candidate with enthusiasm
- clear ability to set the course for the future
- committed to a high level of quality and service excellence
- competent, hardworking and motivated individual, with the enthusiasm it takes
- dedicated team player
- demonstrated ability to perform
- demonstrated commitment to excellence
- diligent, self-motivated
- diplomatic, determined and visionary
- endorse a participative management approach
- energetic, self-motivated professional
- entrepreneurial spirited individual who can initiate and manage change
- excels in a highly independent environment
- exceptionally creative and promotion-oriented executive
- experience working with people of diverse backgrounds
- extremely motivated, proactive and organized with highly effective communication skills
- fresh insights and initiatives
- good interviewing and counselling experience in a helping profession
- handle challenges in a proactive way
- hands-on manager
- high energy individual with an innovative, pro-active approach
- highly skilled professional with a progressive record of achievement
- highly motivated team player with strong interpersonal skills
- independent and goal-oriented
- an individual prepared for revolution rather than evolution

- known for my resourcefulness
- mature and sensitive individual for dealing with...
- no compromise belief in excellence
- possess an entrepreneurial flare
- primary spokesperson and strategist
- progressive, dynamic professional
- proven ability to initiate productive contacts
- quality driven, client-centred professional
- recognized professional in my field
- results-oriented leader
- self-starter who can also work as part of a team
- senior executive with a vision
- sensitive to socio-economic challenges
- skills and talent to meet challenges
- strong sense of self-discipline
- strong conceptual thinker
- strong analytical and interpretive skills
- strong commitment to...
- successful marketing track record
- superior interpersonal skills with a motivating and enabling personality
- talented and creative individual headed for success
- thrives in a collegial environment
- thrives on the opportunity to grow
- top flight professional
- valued contribution to...
- versatile professional
- vital to the success of the organizations continued success and profitability
- well developed ability to conceptualize
- wishing the ultimate challenge

Personal Ability Statements

Ability to:

- achieve results in a competitive and fast paced environment
- act as a broker
- act as a catalyst
- act as a primary spokesperson
- analyze, assess, and recommend proposals
- anticipate industry concerns and positions
- apply skills to projects offering real opportunity for career and professional development
- assess client needs and make referrals
- build team spirit and cohesion
- communicate effectively both within and on behalf of...
- communicate easily at all levels
- communicate fluently in...
- communicate orally and to write clear concise reports
- communicate with a wide range of...
- conduct market research and formulate five year plans
- create a vision for future success and to act as a catalyst
- direct professional staff
- do what it takes
- engage in public outreach activities by giving speeches, organizing and leading seminars, and communicating with media
- ensure growth and diversification
- establish influential relationships
- foster an environment characterized by excellence
- function as an active member of a multi-disciplinary team
- initiate change
- inspire and motivate staff
- interact at a board level
- interact at a senior level
- lead a broad range of initiatives, policy and program development, professional advisement and public education

- lead a team of professionals
- liaise with line ministries and central agencies
- motivate and supervise people
- negotiate effectively
- organize staff
- plan, modify and rationalize
- provide advice on the political ramifications of policy
- provide broad-based leadership, analysis and policy advice on issues affecting the economic, social and legal aspects of...
- provide effective leadership to establish management systems that will ensure integration and co-ordination of...
- provide sound, fact-based, insightful advice on corporate development and growth issues
- provide strategic leadership and direction for long term planning and development
- provide the analytical framework of businesses and their competitive environments
- speak (language)
- successfully manage a dynamic and growing business
- synthesize findings into well substantiated reports
- take the initiative
- thrive in a fast paced environment
- work as part of a team
- work cooperatively, yet work firmly, with
- work effectively with a diverse group of stakeholders
- work effectively with other departments, associations and volunteer boards
- work in a collaborative multi-disciplinary team
- work independently and as a part of a team
- work under pressure, meet deadlines
- work with a wide variety of personalities
- build strong communication channels
- create and achieve marketing plans to achieve sales and profit objectives
- define and gain corporate commitment

- deliver practical, cost effective solutions
- function as a member of a team in a rapidly changing environment
- implement complex systems
- interact effectively with staff
- make significant contributions to continued growth and success
- manage new directions and change
- meet and exceed objectives
- play a pivotal role
- provide strategic and operational leadership to meet new demands
- service as a resource
- take the initiative and anticipate current industry concerns and positions
- undertake all aspects of marketing activities specific to new business activities
- work with private and public sector organizations ranging from grassroots community groups to corporate enterprises
- spot and assess opportunities as they arise
- take advantage of opportunities with minimal planning

Work Environment Phrases

These phrases describe the kind of work environment that you are seeking:

- a thriving, collegial environment
- a highly independent environment
- survive in a fast paced environment
- an environment that fully appreciates
- an organization empowered to assist
- autonomous and multi-faceted professional work environment
- climate that fosters career development
- co-operative work in government and private industry climate
- commitment to quality products and service
- continuous and rapid expansion
- cooperative environment that emphasizes good character
- crown corporation

- dedicated to the discovery, development and marketing of...
- diverse client base
- dynamic organization
- dynamic, cultural and political environment
- endorse a participative management approach
- environment committed to quality management
- evolving world leader
- existing development team
- expanding, independent manufacturer
- fastest growing
- fully modern manufacturing facility producing state of the art....
- genuine opportunities for growth
- growing force in the Canadian market
- high achievement is the norm
- highest standards in service excellence
- known for its quality
- large product manufacturing operation
- leading manufacturing subcontractor
- progressive, innovative leader
- quality driven, client-centred environment
- recognized for its world class expertise

Career/Job Objectives Phrases

- a challenging opportunity
- a challenging and unique opportunity to test my leadership and business management skills
- challenging opportunity to broaden business horizons
- desire to work with a world class organization
- desire to direct the continued growth of...
- desire to be associated with a multi-national company
- desire to be part of a team of top flight professionals
- have the skills and talent to carry out a challenge
- high profile position

- ideal career challenge
- key, senior level position
- opportunity for international travel
- opportunity to successfully manage a very dynamic growing business
- opportunity to manage a growth-oriented team on a national basis
- opportunity to manage a growth-oriented team
- play a key leadership role
- seeking ongoing professional opportunities
- seeking a career growth opportunity
- seeking a high profile position
- seeking the personal reward, challenge and stimulation of working with top level achievers
- seeking the unique opportunity to become an integral part of an executive committee
- seeking future promotional potential
- seeking a unique opportunity
- the challenge of taking an organization successfully through the 1990's
- to apply my experience in the...industry
- to excel in a challenging opportunity
- to work in a challenging and innovative environment
- to make a real contribution and leave a mark on the organization
- to successfully meet diverse challenges
- to be part of a team of talented professionals
- want to actively participate in the exciting cultural and organizational changes...
- want to contribute to the future growth of...
- want to play a lead role
- wish to play a pivotal role
- wish to play a key role in a leading organization

Comprehensive Resource Lists

Appendix C

■

Personal

Profile

Samples

APPENDIX C - PERSONAL PROFILE SAMPLES

The following sample profiles are taken from completed résumés and are categorized for your convenience. Once again, locate the profile that best matches you as you describe yourself – transfer it to your summary profile location and work with it, changing words until the statement really does describe you. Although some of our samples are long, our rule is to keep it short! But, an overriding rule is that your résumé is your résumé. We can only advise!

Profile samples can be found for:

Administrator/Administrative Assistant/Secretary

- A self-motivated, energetic, outgoing individual who has the ability to develop high morale within a team environment. Conscientious and dedicated worker with experience in administrative support services. Bilingual interpersonal communication skills capable of initiating a strong rapport with clients, co-workers and management.
- Bilingual senior administrative professional with ten years of broad spectrum management experience emphasizing an entrepreneurial leadership style. Key strengths are in program design, implementation and evaluation, facilitation of an empowered, total quality environment and expertise in project management. Hands-on professional challenged by an organization seeking an assertive, results-oriented leader capable of enhancing and expanding the quality and quantity of service delivery.
- Energetic, results-oriented corporate executive assistant with significant leadership, organizational and administrative strengths. Confident strategic thinker and problem solver with excellent communication and interpersonal skills, well suited to a fast pace, time dependent environment. Seeking new organizational management challenges that test my expertise.
- Dependable, well organized, team-oriented employee with excellent organizational skills and ability to follow detailed instructions. Able to work with a wide variety of people and to provide warmth and support as needed. Practical-oriented person seeking new challenges.
- Conscientious, self-directed office administrator and senior accounting clerk with progressively responsible experience. Computer literate with key skills in generating financial statements, reconciliation of monthly statements, preparation of cash flow analysis and management of purchasing and inventory control. Seeking new challenges in an office environment.
- Conscientious, resourceful individual with excellent ability to follow instructions, implement and complete tasks. Good communication and interpersonal skills for effective teamwork. Hard working and competent worker with experience in a variety of environments.

Communications/Public Relations

- A dedicated, hard working and versatile corporate relations professional. Key strengths in project management and the hospitality industry with a strong emphasis on customer development and service. Demonstrated experience in sales and marketing, financial management, and budget planning. A proven leader with excellent teambuilding, communication, and organizational skills who is totally committed to my customers and employees.

- A strongly motivated, experienced and results-oriented communications specialist offering production of print materials from concept through writing and/or editing to finished product for presentation. Excellent organization and co-ordination strengths complemented by the ability to develop and sustain sound working relationships. Seeking challenging opportunities to bring orderly thought processes and creative talents to written communication projects.
- Creative promotional strategist who excels in establishing new markets. Calculating risk player who explores new alternatives to accomplishing goals. Seasoned hands-on business management specialist with a strong team leadership style enhanced by superior strengths in utilizing experience and resourcefulness in realizing goals. Seeking challenging position that would profitably exploit my talents and energy.
- Enterprising, innovative communications professional with significant organizational talent. Creative, resourceful, independent thinker and problem solver with excellent interpersonal skills and an eye for detail. Extensive experience in a flexible, action-oriented, multi-task environment.
- Highly creative, bilingual communications professional with significant strengths in short and long-term communications. Strong expertise in planning, media writing, public and media relations as well as television production. Strong conceptual thinker with an ability to foresee trends and needs. Able to undertake simultaneous projects and adapt quickly to changing priorities.
- Imaginative, innovative professional with a high degree of expertise in the communications and promotion field. Creative and charismatic in interactions with others coupled with an appreciation for an action-oriented, multi-task employment environment.
- Results-oriented communicator with key strengths in planning and executing projects, handling media relations and initiating/organizing activities and events. Keen ability to make decisions and follow projects through to completion. Deal well with unexpected and critical events. Effective ability to handle a variety of responsibilities and work in a self-directed manner.

Customer Service Management

- An exceptional, results-oriented professional with significant experience and expertise in challenging, fast-paced environments. A high achiever with excellent analytical, communication and business process skills. Seeking managerial responsibilities in a customer-oriented investment services firm.

- Conscientious, customer services-oriented print professional with over ten years of progressively responsible experience in offset printing. Well developed communication skills for the identification of customer needs. Well organized with ability to complete difficult assignments and work well under the pressure of tight timelines. Seeking new opportunities in the printing field.

- Customer service-oriented, management professional and entrepreneur with strong personal initiative and dedication to rural community development. Extensive experience in venture capital as well as development of strategic business planning, personnel and administrative management. Sensitive team player with well developed skills for interfacing with clients, public and private agencies, government, peers and superiors. Skilled in financial management of large scale account portfolios. Seeking opportunity to utilize unique background and skills.

- Highly experienced customer service management professional possessing a proven track record of developing, achieving and maintaining excellent customer and employee satisfaction while safeguarding and enhancing company interests.

- Highly self-motivated individual who enjoys the challenges of problem solving. A team player, implementing new ideas in business and providing superior customer service. Extensive experience in sales and marketing within the commercial and retail sales environment.

- Seasoned customer service-oriented sales professional. Significant expertise and operational management including marketing, finance and human resources. Seeking a position which will utilize my skills and expertise.

Engineer/Research Scientist

- A highly motivated professional with strengths in research, evaluation, planning and training. Possesses superior analytical and problem solving skills with extensive background in univariate and multivariate statistical analyses. Over sixteen years experience in use of mainframe statistical computer packages (SAS, SPSSX, BMDP). Strengths in planning, organization, and establishing cooperative and productive relationships. Able to work with a team or independently. Looking for a creative and challenging work environment.
- A professional engineer possessing extensive senior management expertise in diverse operating environments. Demonstrated proficiency in the integration of people and resources to maximize productivity and increase production. Seeking challenging career opportunity to utilize unique combination of skills and expertise to make things happen.
- A research and development professional who possesses excellent expertise in several mathematical and physical sciences with significant experience in academic research and a specialization in the application of mathematical methods to industrial problems encompassing in particular, modeling and algorithm development. Additional attributes include proficiency in R&D project management and rationalization, budget and proposal preparation, technical liaison complemented by excellent interpersonal, organization and motivational skills.
- Highly motivated, results-oriented Engineering Professional with demonstrated expertise in Just-In-Time, Total Quality Management and ISO-9000 standards and their implications in the areas of operational analysis, cost reduction, productivity and quality. Seeking professional challenges which enable significant contribution to corporate goals.
- Multilingual, highly motivated and collaborative scientist who likes to work within a multi-disciplinary environment. Skilled teacher with the ability to develop conceptual frameworks and theories, apply theories to indoor air quality problems, develop concise yet high quality technical reports, and translate documents into French, German and Russian.
- Seasoned researcher and project co-ordinator in the medical and health sciences field. Expertise includes bio-electric climatology applied to air quality and medical respiratory problems. Strengths in irreversible thermodynamics with applications in biophysical chemistry complemented by numerical mathematics, applied probability and statistics skills. Fluent in French and German with basic knowledge of Russian.

Executive Management

- A management executive with expertise in marketing, communications, and program design and delivery. Highly motivated and innovative with excellent organization, supervisory and presentation skills. A demonstrated ability to address issues and achieve results.
- A senior executive with extensive experience in construction product sales, promotion and dealer support work. Technically-oriented professional, with proven success in new product introduction.
- A Senior General Manager with extensive experience in managing operations, finances and personnel within the commercial and retail sales environment. Demonstrated expertise in hiring, training, motivating and terminating staff, market identification and sales projections, general budget preparation and overall financial management to ensure the best possible bottom line results.
- An accomplished executive with excellent communications skills, and proven ability in problem solving, team building, motivational training, client service, and sales management.
- Creative, flexible and articulate senior executive. Possess demonstrated analytical and organizational skills. Well developed and proven management and consulting expertise in the area of business analysis, TQM, strategic, financial, and market planning. Able to work with a team or independently. Enjoy an environment of creativity and challenge.
- Extensive and diverse background in senior management positions within the hospitality industry. Very effective in maintaining or exceeding profits relative to budget projection, without compromising customer service or satisfaction. Committed to teamwork and development of a sense of professional pride and self-worth within the hospitality and service industry.
- Extensive and diverse background in senior management positions involving marketing, administration, operations, public relations and human resources. Able to develop and maintain budget projections without compromising service or customer satisfaction. A results-oriented professional committed to personal and organizational success.

Financial Management

- Accomplished, energetic financial manager with an excellent combination of formal education and practical hands-on experience in business management and accounting. Highly motivated, hard working and committed to quality, integrity and profitability.
- Conscientious, reliable individual with a good working knowledge of basic accounting principals complemented by a solid customer service perspective. Mature and responsible work orientation approach to problem solving, with an ability to take the initiative and lead small projects. Seeking opportunities that integrate university studies and previous work experience.
- Experienced financial professional with expertise in analyzing, developing and implementing computer systems. Proficient hands-on developer of spreadsheet and DBase applications. Team leader committed to developing and motivating staff to meet deadlines on time and within budget.
- Highly motivated, results-oriented, take charge professional with key leadership strengths in organizational development, communications, and financial management. Extensive entrepreneurial, strategic planning and leadership experience in business start-up management and community development. Seeking a challenging career opportunity to utilize my unique combination of skills and expertise in a fast paced working environment.
- Pragmatic, seasoned executive with a solid background and progressive experience complemented by strong strategic planning, organizational and negotiation skills. Excellent leadership and general management strengths, with a recognized track record of success in supervising and leading management staff in the attainment of business targets. Seeking a key role in a challenging new environment.
- Results-oriented professional manager/leader. Experienced in all aspects of business and not-for-profit association management. Hands on manager who develops effective subordinates within a team management style. Skilled in operations administration, leadership, communication, marketing, financial management, human resources, planning, corporate reorganization, client service, and government relations.

Food/Hospitality

- Highly skilled food services specialist with a solid customer service orientation and key strengths in large scale "homestyle" meal preparation and specialty baking for varied client groups. Seasoned supervisor able to supervise and manage staff, estimate and manage inventory within budgetary guidelines. Seeking new challenges that utilize organizational and creative abilities.
- Seasoned bilingual operations manager with over six years of experience in retail and food services. Key strengths in communications with the ability to train and develop staff, and manage customer relations, budget and inventory control. Strong initiator seeking new challenges.
- Twelve years supervisory/management experience in the Food Service Industry. Work conscientiously and productively to increase profitability and maintain a high standard of customer service. Excellent record of reliability and dependability.

General Business

- Exceptional leader with proven strengths in communication, team building, interpersonal skills and pro-active customer relationships. Comprehensive experience in administration, budget control, human resources, operations and strategic planning. Professional manager seeking challenging opportunities to contribute to efficient work practices.
- Hands-on, value driven, team leader and astute problem solver, possessing superior financial, communication and interpersonal skills. Achievement-oriented supportive manager seeking new organizational challenges that test and augment management expertise.
- Highly motivated professional with a proven track record as a strategic planner, motivator and team builder. An innovative and creative leader with excellent interpersonal, communication and management skills. A visionary with a keen ability to identify and assess changing conditions in an organization, and match resources to short and long term priorities.
- Highly self-motivated individual who enjoys the challenges of problem solving. A team player, implementing new ideas in business and providing superior customer service. Extensive experience in sales and marketing within the commercial and retail sales environment.
- Independent, self-reliant individual with good business abilities complemented by a keen commitment to customer satisfaction. Eager to be fully active and seeking new employment challenges.

- Keen, responsible, and diligent individual with many years of work experience in a variety of environments. Strong organizational skills with a systematic approach to accomplishing tasks. Strong customer service orientation. Seeking new challenges.
- Professional business leader with key strengths in financial management, strategic planning, organizational development, computerization projects. Possesses an extensive background which includes significant accomplishments in housing, education and child care within a cross-cultural, board-based governance environment.
- Visionary, diplomatic professional with proven administrative and financial skills; good abilities in oral and written communication; insightful problem solver; effective leader.

Health Care Management

- Experienced, professional manager specializing in the health/service sector. Committed to integrity, pursuing a vision focusing on solutions and turning complex problems into opportunities. Strong analytical problem solving, negotiation and decision making skills with extensive Canadian and International experience in Health and Rehabilitation. Seeking highly responsible management challenges.
- Highly skilled, results-oriented health care generalist with experience in diverse organizational functions encompassing human, material and financial accountability. Able to undertake leadership roles utilizing demonstrated analytical problem solving skills. Well organized with good communication and interpersonal skills. Seeking an opportunity to contribute as a team player.
- Well-organized and effective health care management professional with key strengths in crisis intervention, assessment, planning, implementation and evaluation. Extensive leadership skills in a multi-disciplinary environment. Seeking challenging opportunity to use skills and expertise.
- Results-oriented, visionary health care professional with extensive expertise in the critical analysis of issues, strategic planning and administrative management. Conscientious team leader with strong continuous quality improvement perspective. Seeking new challenges in health care.

Hospitality Management

- Highly self-motivated manager with extensive background in the service industry. Demonstrated expertise in exceeding budgeted profit performance while providing superior customer service. Excels in taking on new challenges with proven skills in recruiting, training, motivating staff, overall financial management and general administration.
- Highly self-motivated professional with extensive and diverse background in management positions within the service industry. Demonstrated expertise in promoting, marketing; hiring, training, and motivating staff; budget preparation; and overall financial management to ensure the best possible result. Enjoys the challenge of problem solving, being a team leader, implementing new ideas and providing a superior customer service.
- Hospitality professional with key skills in operational assessment, financial analysis and personnel management. Committed to the highest quality of customer service and complemented by comprehensive food and beverage experience. Seeking career opportunities to challenge skills and expertise.
- Multilingual, highly self-motivated, hands-on General Manager, with a diverse and international background in executive, and hospitality management. Demonstrated experience in exceeding budgeted profit performance while providing superior customer service. Committed to team work and professional pride. Seeking challenging career opportunity to utilize unique combination of skills and expertise in a fast paced working environment.
- Multilingual hospitality professional with extensive expertise in food and beverage management complemented by solid foundation in European professional training. Excellent customer service orientation and ability to plan, co-ordinate and to meet, exceed unique social events, conferences, workshops and seminars. Seeking challenging career opportunity to utilize skills and expertise.
- Multilingual European trained hospitality professional with extensive management of food and beverage operations. Total customer service management philosophy complemented by solid organizational abilities and proven skills in financial management, recruitment and motivating staff. Seeking challenging career opportunity to utilize skills and abilities.

- Results-oriented General Manager who thrives on the challenge of continuous improvement in a customer service environment. Proven skills in project management, training, recruitment and communication. Demonstrated expertise in operations analysis, systems development, loss prevention and risk management. Dedicated to maintaining and improving customer service without compromising profitability.

Human Resources Management

- An accomplished personnel/administrative professional with extensive experience in public sector, manufacturing and service industries. Detail-oriented with a commitment to high standards. Seeking professional challenges and career opportunities to become a key contributor in a team-oriented environment.
- A highly motivated seasoned professional with negotiation and motivational abilities, who enjoys a challenging result-oriented position. Proficient in human resources management including motivation, evaluation, training and supervision. Strong analytical skills in a demanding decision making setting.
- A highly motivated manager with superior analytical skills gained through above average organization and determination. Strong interpersonal, negotiation and communication skills. Well developed problem solving and decision making capabilities. Proficient in human resource management and delivery of quality customer service. A professional willing to learn new concepts and techniques, demonstrated ability to perform accurate work in pressure situations.
- Dynamic professional with proven experience in the field of human resources including training and development. Well developed abilities to plan, organize, and implement successful completion of small business starts, business related projects, and fundraising events. Independent, motivated and results-oriented with excellent follow through capabilities.
- Employee Benefits Specialist, able to independently analyze and resolve out of the ordinary and unexpected problems acting with cleverness and timeliness. Confident thinker with facilitative, communicative, interpersonal and presentation skills developed in an employee benefits environment. Able negotiator sensitive to the needs of internal and external customers.
- Human Resource Generalist able to independently analyze and resolve unexpected problems acting with cleverness and timeliness. Confident thinker with facilitative, communicative, interpersonal and presentation skills developed in an employee benefits environment. Able negotiator sensitive to the needs of internal and external customers.

Management

- A dynamic, results-oriented manager/administrator with expertise and experience in a T.Q.M./Continuous Quality Improvement environment. Comprehensive strengths in strategic planning and the management of change, systems analysis, project and financial management, and program evaluation. Superior interpersonal skills as exhibited through the co-ordination and negotiation/mediation of multiple projects/assignments. Seeking opportunities in organizations facing challenging comprehensive change.
- A highly skilled manager of diverse organizational functions. A strategic planner who takes initiative and is innovative, creative, and meets goals. A leader who is a trainer, facilitator and team builder. A bottom line manager who increases productivity and organizational effectiveness. Highly organized with good communication and interpersonal skills.
- A progressive manager with extensive experience and diversified background. Highly motivated and innovative combined with excellent people and presentation skills. Results-oriented and demonstrated versatility in achieving organizational goals.
- A senior manager for over 20 years, in buying, marketing and human resources. Expert communicator and motivator. Imaginative, pioneering business attitude with a pragmatic approach to constraints and opportunities.
- An experienced general management and plant operations professional effective at organizing and directing production/profit centres in a participatory management environment. Goal-oriented with excellent communication and leadership skills complemented by a working knowledge of financial reports and strong technical abilities in the food industry. Career objectives are management opportunities in food and related industries.
- An innovative manager with a positive, results-oriented approach to meeting objectives and problem solving. A successful track record in building and maintaining profitable sales territories. An effective negotiator utilizing strong oral and written communication skills. An organized planner able to schedule priorities and manage time efficiently.
- Broad and versatile experienced manager in departmental administration, liaison and recruitment. Strong interpersonal, negotiation and communication skills. Well developed problem solving and decision making capabilities. Knowledgeable in plant safety, security, labour relations and human resource management.

Marketing

- An Entrepreneur with more than 15 years' experience focused on Marketing and Sales. Key elements of expertise are in achieving simultaneous maximization of market share and profitability, excellent interpersonal and communication skills and superior team-building talent. Hands-on professional who enjoys the challenge of an aggressive, results-oriented total quality environment.
- Accomplished marketing and visual merchandising professional with extensive experience and expertise in the management of large and small scale retail enterprises. Superior strengths in aggressive sales techniques, dynamic marketing, power visual merchandising and quality customer service dedicated to bottom line profitability and accountability. Seeking challenge in a sales and marketing, or retail opportunity.
- Achievement driven marketing specialist with well developed market planning skills, resourceful problem solving expertise and a proven track record in sales. Hands-on professional who enjoys the challenge of a results-oriented environment. Seeking a leadership opportunity to utilize marketing and business expertise to meet and exceed corporate objectives.
- Dynamic marketing and advertising professional experienced with multi-level co-ordination and presentation in new product development. Proven operations manager possessing consumer driven business expertise. Achievement-oriented and bottom line focused. Seeking new and challenging opportunities.
- Professional manager with a solid background in marketing, transportation, quality control and processing. Self-motivated to provide innovative answers to complex problems in a low risk/low margin industry. Seeking opportunity to focus skills and expertise in a challenging environment.
- Professional marketing executive with proven track record in sales and management in a fast paced customer service environment. Young, open minded leader who believes all activities revolve around looking after the customer. Enthusiastic individual interested in meeting new challenges.
- Results-oriented senior executive with key strengths in creative merchandising and marketing skills within a multi-department retail environment. Strong customer service focus complemented by problem solving expertise. Seeking creative challenges to utilize expertise.

Non-profit Management

- A results-driven community organizational Executive Director with key strengths in the management of both professional and lay staff in all aspects of advocacy, promotion and fund-raising. Possesses the ability to portray the needs of the organization to the population at large. Seeking challenges to utilize skills and expertise in a community setting.
- Experienced professional with key strengths in organizational management and significant leadership. Accomplishments in volunteer co-ordination, training, and specialized research. Self-motivated, analytical thinker with effective and strong interpersonal skills. Seeking challenging opportunities to utilize skills and strengths.
- Enthusiastic, self-directed and innovative team player with proven track record of accomplishments in business development and project co-ordination. Strong customer service orientation complemented by bottom line focus. Dedicated to seeking opportunities to utilize organizational skills in a people-oriented environment.
- Highly energetic, people-oriented individual with excellent organizational and administrative qualities. Demonstrated and proven strengths in research and development of ground level projects, action-oriented problem solving skills, refined reflective skills and creative thinking.
- Project-oriented visionary and highly energetic professional sales manager and fund-raiser with a keen sense of the marketplace. Demonstrates high level of competence in communicating, promotional advertising, training programs, introducing customer appreciation procedures, developing revenue and operating budgets, trouble shooting and team building.
- Resourceful, versatile executive with eight years of senior management experience, proactive marketing, and a demonstrated ability to get the job done. An innovative achiever with excellent interpersonal skills and who thrives on teamwork and challenge.
- Seasoned cultural professional with strong administrative, planning, organizational and negotiating skills. Demonstrated record of responsible management and financial stability while fostering artistic growth. Achievement-oriented leader, astute listener and analyst who enjoys developing a self-reliant team to address creative and financial challenges. Visionary, diplomatic management professional with proven administrative and financial skills; good abilities in oral and written communication; insightful problem solver; effective leader.

- Self-motivated bilingual professional with key strengths in management, co-ordination, training in multi-cultural settings. Results-oriented catalyst with strong problem solving, negotiation and decision making skills, complemented by extensive sales and marketing within a non-profit environment.

Operations Management

- A General Manager experienced in managing operations, finances and personnel within the commercial and retail sales environment. With demonstrated expertise in hiring, training, motivating and terminating staff, market identification and sales projections, general budget preparation, and overall financial management to ensure the best possible bottom line results. A highly self-motivated individual, who enjoys the challenges of problem solving, being a team leader, implementing new ideas in business, and providing a superior customer service.

- An innovative operations and customer service professional, with the skills required to successfully implement change in a dynamic environment. Strong leadership, analytical and communication skills combined with a decisive problem solver. Seeking an opportunity to make a significant contribution in a team medium.

- Conscientious, responsible, hands-on professional with extensive experience in production management, sales, engineering and quality assurance. People and customer-oriented, humanistic approach to problem solving with keen ability to develop trust in an encouraging and supportive environment. Strong team orientation with well developed customer service skills.

- Experienced operations and production professional with keen ability to analyze and implement new ideas in retail and plant settings. Extensive track record in training and development with demonstrated ability to co-ordinate operations in a fast paced environment.

- Professional pro-active maintenance manager with specialization in plastic blow moulding, high speed bottling, canning and processing equipment. Demonstrated expertise in all phases of building maintenance. Excellent interpersonal skills complemented by advanced team building and human relations strengths.

- Progressive plant operations professional with extensive business management skills. Self-starter and quick learner who can work in multi-varied roles. Effective interpersonal and communication skills enhance a team oriented management style. Well developed skills to elicit participation. Hands-on manager seeking a career opportunity to be a member of a dedicated, management team.

Policy Analysis

- Accomplished professional with key strengths in fields of economics and political science complemented by a solid foundation in the analysis of legal and legislative issues. Energetic and thorough with excellent interpersonal skills for participation in a team environment, seeking challenges which provide for key goals in political, economic and social change.

- Experienced, professional manager specializing in social policy and research. Committed to integrity, pursuing a vision and turning complex problems into opportunities. Strong analytical problem solving, negotiation and decision making skills with extensive Canadian and International experience in Health and Rehabilitation. Seeking continued progressive research, policy and academic challenges.

- Highly motivated administration manager, with specific expertise and proven experience in the examination, design and implementation of Business Accounting Systems for Manufacturing, Contracting, Retail and Service Industries. Trained in Legislation and Policy on Provincial Tax Statutes and Federal Taxation.

- Skilled professional with fourteen years of program management and policy development experience within a multi-disciplinary environment. Creative and innovative manager with an intuitive ability to complement an organizations changing environment. Seeking an opportunity to meet challenges while contributing to the bottom line.

Project Management

- Experienced project management and building planning professional possessing demonstrated organizational abilities. Proven skills in project co-ordination and crisis management. Accomplished in providing on time and on budget project completions. Self-motivated analytical thinker with strong communication skills.

- Professional manager with responsible experience in project management, systems improvement and computerized accounting. Strong team builder with system skills who effectively solves problems and implements solutions.

Retail Management

- Agriculture graduate with extensive farm management experience as well as managing operations, finances and personnel in the commercial and retail sales setting. Demonstrated expertise in human resource management, general budget preparations, sales projections and overall financial management which achieved top customer service. A highly self-motivated individual who enjoys the challenge of problem solving, implementing new ideas in business and works effectively on boards and committees. An active participant in many community organizations and clubs.

- Experience gained by 18 years of management in several areas of the retail sector. Effective in maintaining and controlling all costs relative to budget projections. Committed to developing a team dedicated to sales volume without compromising customer services or satisfaction. Seeking a sales intensive position where my skills with people, both customer and staff, can be used to their potential.

- Extensive administrative management experience working within retail and warehouse environments. Strong financial skills with demonstrated marketing skills and experience. Proven initiative, with the ability to motivate staff in order to effectively achieve objectives in a given time frame.

- Fluently bilingual hands-on general manager with extensive experience in the retail sector. Demonstrated expertise in operations analysis, systems development, loss prevention, risk management recruitment and training. Dedicated to maintaining customer service without compromising profitability.

- Retail professional with a positive, success-oriented attitude complemented by thirteen years of experience in management and supervision of daily operations and financial planning. Skilled in meeting management challenges of a retail chain of multi-geographic locations.

- Seasoned administrative manager with extensive experience obtained within a retail environment. Excellent financial knowledge of planning, analyzing, and evaluating plans. Dedicated team player with proven interpersonal skills applied in accomplishing department and company objectives.

Sales And Marketing/Customer Service

- A dedicated and conscientious sales manager with a proven track record and extensive management background in recruiting, negotiation, interpersonal and communication skills. Excellent interpersonal strengths with highly developed leadership qualities. Well organized team player with the ability to work independently.

- A professional with more than 20 years' experience focused primarily on purchasing, customer relations, sales development and administration. Particularly recognized for strengths in planning, organization, establishing co-operative and productive relationships and a substantial and diversified knowledge base. Hands-on administrative manager, resourceful, proficient in project management and demonstrates grace under pressure.

- A seasoned marketing and sales professional with 10 years' progressive experience in the food production and service industry. A multidimensional manager with superior strengths in cooperatively maximizing sales and staff potential, market analysis, and regional distribution strategies, creative training programs and effective team building. Hands-on professional who enjoys the challenge of an aggressive, results-oriented total quality environment.

- Agriculture graduate with extensive farm management experience as well as managing operations, finances and personnel in the commercial and retail sales setting. Demonstrated expertise in human resource management, general budget preparations, sales projections and overall financial management which achieved top customer service. A highly self-motivated individual who enjoys the challenge of problem solving, implementing new ideas in business and works effectively on boards and committees. An active participant in many community organizations and clubs.

- Creative sales and marketing professional with significant management experience in challenging, fast paced environments. Highly motivated with strong leadership and administrative strengths supported by good communication and public relations skills. Keen business development sensitivity including evaluation and goal setting for bottom line performance in start-up opportunities. Exceptional analytical skills that help strengthen a successful win/win negotiation style.

- Dependable, co-operative, team-oriented individual with keen customer service sensitivity. Excellent organizational skills for hands-on co-ordination of tasks. Seeking work opportunity that utilizes skills and experience.

Social Services Management

- Accomplished professional possessing executive level expertise in social service delivery. Skilled legal practitioner with ability to address practical issues with empathy. Demonstrated skills in planning and management, grant writing, advocacy, mediation, program design, budgeting and research.
- Excellent skills and abilities in crisis, stress and anger management including assessment, counselling and client monitoring.
- Experienced human relations professional with key strengths in conflict resolution, mentoring and group facilitation. A solution-centered and sensitive counsellor, great communicator, and team player. Dedicated to the personal development of individuals and groups. Seeking employment in a personal, professional and disciplined environment.
- Good working knowledge of a number of key justice department and social services programs including the Fine Option Program, the Community Service Order Program, Parole Supervision and Community Assessments.
- Proven proficiency in crisis management and conflict resolution through effective use of issues identification, mediation and sound decision making skills.
- Seasoned crisis counselling and mediating professional with excellent skills in problem identification, analyses and conflict resolution. Addresses advocacy issues with a humanistic management approach.
- Significant knowledge of the corrections system with the ability to provide assessment, counselling and treatment referral for men and women involved with drug and alcohol abuse.
- Skilled in family violence and abuse counselling including sexual, mental, physical and chemical, providing individual, family and group counselling.
- Solid foundation and working knowledge of vocational rehabilitation, health, disabilities, child welfare, and employment equity.
- Solid team work skills with the ability to work with a multi-disciplinary team of professionals to develop, deliver and evaluate social service programming.
- Solid working knowledge of client admission and release procedures including processing, screening, interviewing, co-ordinating space and working with external agencies to meet client needs.

Technical/Manufacturing/Engineering

- A hands-on manager with more than 20 years' experience in technical and engineering organizations. Knowledgeable in mechanical, electrical, hydraulic and pneumatic systems, as well as manufacturing tooling, equipment and quality assurance. Experienced in U.S.A. and Canadian Government procurement practices. Conducted international marketing activities, market research and business development assessment for engineered products and services.
- Extensive and diverse background in product management within the construction industry. Effective in maintaining cost control relative to budget projections. Committed to teamwork in a departmental setting.
- Progressive manufacturing Operations Professional with a strong management style, enhanced by technical competence, financial acumen and successful project leadership. Hands-on manager who enjoys the challenge of problem solving in a results-oriented, total quality environment. Seeking to participate as a member of a dedicated and skilled management team in an organization and be part of its success story.
- Progressive manufacturing Operations Professional with a strong management style, enhanced by technical competence, financial acumen and successful project leadership. Hands-on manager who enjoys the challenge of problem solving in a results-oriented, total quality environment. Seeking new operational challenge.
- Seasoned professional with superior skills and expertise in prototype mechanical design. Extensive, and successful research and supervisory experience with solid reputation for innovation and productivity. Qualified and comfortable in working with manufacturing and marketing professionals to develop commercially viable products. Seeking continued creative design challenges.
- A committed and experienced manufacturing professional with extensive experience and demonstrated ability to efficiently manage production resources to achieve organization targets. Utilizes hands-on knowledge to continuously improve production processes in a just-in-time manufacturing environment with a focus on customer satisfaction. A teambuilding and employee motivation specialist with strong communication and interpersonal skills.

Training And Development

Business Leadership

- Creative and innovative trainer and facilitator with intuitive ability to assist organizations in their changing environments. Skilled professional with fourteen years of program management and policy development within a multi-disciplinary field. Sensitive to the effects change will have socially, economically and environmentally.
- Innovative training and development professional with project management background. Proven expertise in competency based training, adult education and community development. Strong interpersonal, problem solving and teamwork skills gained and demonstrated through challenging work projects and extensive community and board activities.

Cross Cultural

- Accomplished cross cultural professional with superior strengths in training, counselling and management. Bottom line focused, well organized and action-oriented problem solver who thrives on innovative challenges. Excellent interpersonal skills in diverse working environments. Seeking challenges utilizing comprehensive skills and expertise.
- Self-motivated bilingual professional with key strengths in management, co-ordinating and training in multi-cultural settings. Results-oriented catalyst with strong problem solving, negotiation and decision making skills, complemented by extensive sales and marketing skills within a training environment.

Health Care

- A nursing professional with a strong background in clinical and classroom teaching. Extensive experience in curriculum development, program planning, implementation and evaluation. Well organized, high energy professional seeking an opportunity in nursing education.
- Innovative, proactive and dynamic leader skilled in communicating throughout the organization. Experienced professional manager specializing in program design, project management and organizational development. Looking for challenges utilizing skills to contribute to an organization.

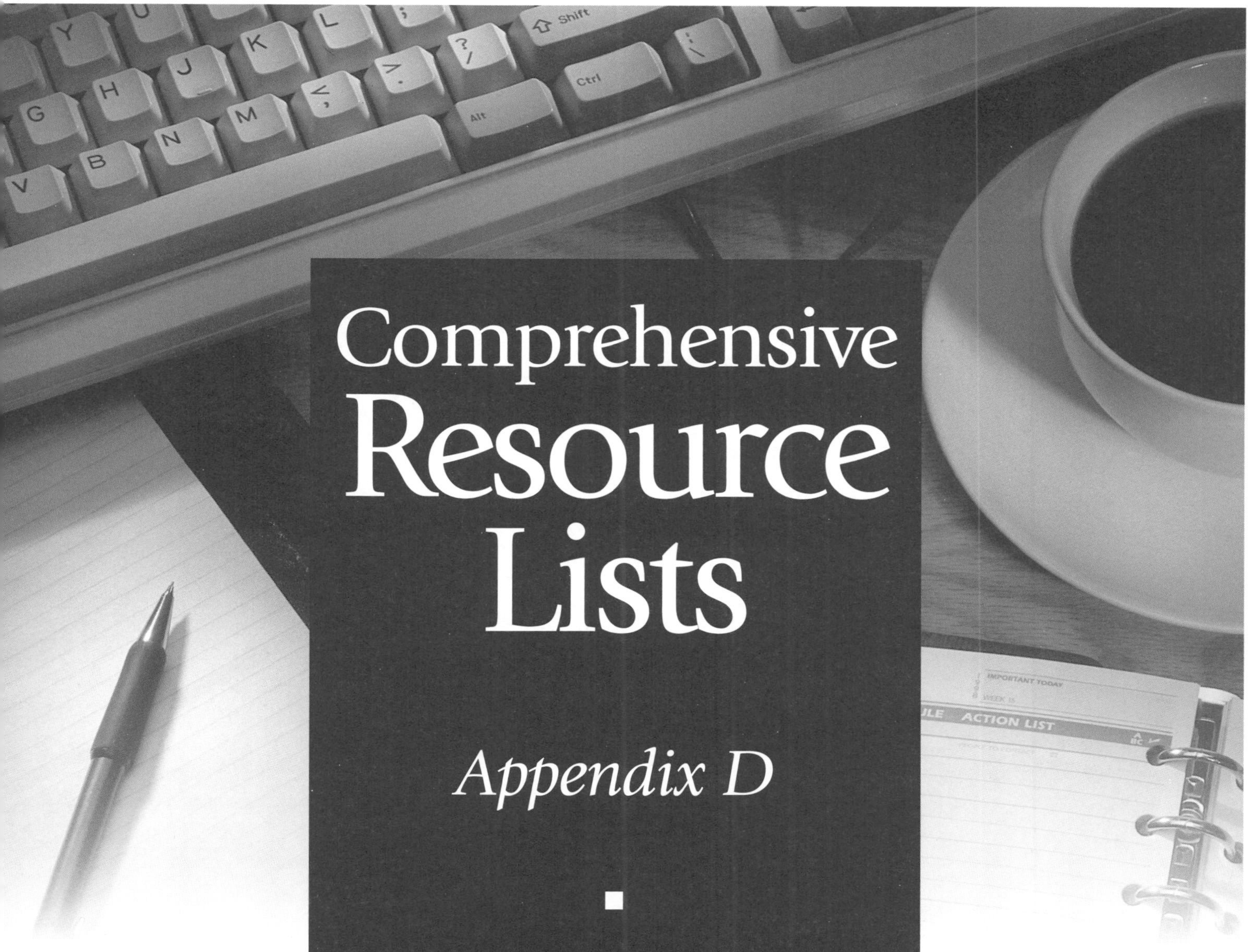

Comprehensive Resource Lists

Appendix D

■

Accomplishments

APPENDIX D - ACCOMPLISHMENTS

Accomplishments can be found for:

Accounting/Financial Management

- Analyzed and corrected deficiencies in general ledger accounts, substantially improving the quality of financial management and reducing audit fees by $15,000 in the first year.
- Assumed responsibilities of corporate controller for an extended period. Communicated with divisions, established report requirements and deadlines and issued monthly and quarterly financial statements, budgets and profit plans in a timely manner.
- By undertaking the additional responsibilities for the completion of working papers for year end financial statements, was able to decrease external accounting audit costs.
- Co-ordinated the financial reporting and management information requirements for six separate companies, comprised of up to twenty divisions, using a manual accounting system.
- Designed, developed, negotiated and implemented an electronic payment system resulting in more efficient payment and improved company receivables.
- Identified and investigated discrepancies in financial accounts resulting in overpayments, short shipments and unbilled revenues.
- Pursuant to the sale of the company to a large multinational, redesigned the management reporting, budgeting and financial statement presentations to comply with the new parent requirements.
- Responsible for $4 million in accounts receivable which were maintained and current. Implemented new procedures resulting in cost and time savings.
- Revitalized six businesses and stabilized their cash flow problems resulting in the retention of over 30 jobs.
- Successfully developed cycling collection methods to reduce delinquent accounts, stimulating corporate cash flow.

Business Process Re-Engineering/Total Quality Management

- Conducted organizational assessment, identified operational issues, conceived and implemented a strategic plan for improvements which resulted in increased profitability within one year.
- Developed, implemented and led a Total Quality Management program which greatly improved customer orientation and became the role model for the corporation.
- Developed a quality assurance system, eliminating errors in delivery of supplies.
- In the continuous search for excellence, using cost containment and analytical forte; researched, developed and qualified sources and processes ensuring profitability results in excess of one million dollars.
- Introduced a Total Quality Management program to a manufacturing environment focusing on piece work, resulting in dramatic improvements in inventory usage and long-term customer satisfaction.
- Pioneered a customer satisfaction and quality insurance program including SPC and QFD resulting in expanded sales of $2.5 million.
- Spearheaded and implemented team plans to improve customer satisfaction and product reliability resulting in the achievement of national status recognition.
- Successfully supervised a staff of engineers and technologists in a specialized scientific research environment to achieve unique and measurable production improvements.
- Using strong analytical and interpersonal skills, reorganized a department into teams, improving productivity, reducing unit costs and processing time (30%) resulting in an immediate and continued annual savings.
- Utilizing continuous quality improvement techniques with twelve staff, reduced invoice turnaround which resulting in capturing of discounts and reducing inventory shrinkage.

Computer Systems/Information Technology

- Analyzed system needs and assisted design, development and implementation of customized accounting system to replace an outdated manual system.
- Assisted in identifying, purchasing and implementing new computerized equipment for the milling operation increasing efficiency by an immediate 20%.
- Conducted a feasibility study to determine the cost, benefits and implementation requirements for an integrated logistics support system. Considered hardware, software, facility, staffing and training requirements. Study identified high risks and recommended a no go decision.
- Converted manual supply stockroom accounting to a computer application, reducing inventory investment by 50%, shrinkage to less than 1% and reducing overall stockroom labour hours.
- Created and implemented a computerized territory account planning system that facilitated the tracking, analysis and planning of both the specific geographic market plans and the annual corporate market plan.
- Developed and implemented a computer strategy for a large government department which resulted in the use of computer tendering networked with regional offices. Project was completed on time and under budget.
- Established a computerized schedule reporting system contributing to increased productivity and the improvement of order deadline efficiency by 15%.
- Successfully identified and made recommendations on office automation directions for a major public utility with multiple incompatible computer systems, including opportunities for significant cost savings using office systems as a basis for system re-engineering labour intensive clerical tasks such as overdue accounts notices.
- Successfully managed and installed major computer program revisions requiring intense research, planning, and consultation with key stakeholders at all levels resulting in minimum disruption during the implementation phase.

Customer Service

- Conducted and moderated confidential customer focus group meetings which resulted in the compilations of information regarding client expectations.
- Led and pioneered a customer satisfaction and quality insurance program including QFD, resulting the expansion of sales by $2.5 million.
- Launched a consumer appreciation department resulting in an improved business/community relations.
- Planned and undertook a marketing and personal contact campaign which largely increased customer base through new and returned customers.
- Recognized for customer service orientation and ability to plan, co-ordinate and to meet unique needs, varied social events, conferences, workshops and seminars.
- Through ability to recognize and act on market opportunities, was able to improve customer/supplier relationship at a bulk dealership resulting in a significant fuel, lubricant and farm supply increase.

Engineer/Environment/Research Science

- Conceptualized and improved yield by 2% in a large processing plant by introducing concepts to refine the technology.
- Designed an optimal numerical scheme to determine density distribution in rocks by sound travel time tomography.
- Developed environmental impact assessment, reclamation and rehabilitation programs, and managed these through licensing process.
- Developed accurate and efficient methods to obtain solutions and catastrophic pointsignition and bio-mass systems.
- Developed and modified matrix solvers arising in various applications such as finite elements and finite difference methods.
- Improved and modified variational methods to solve problems, in control theory and systems.
- Improved by 100% the efficiency of numerical methods to determine flow regimes and fractions in fluid flowing in pipes by gamma densitometers.
- Pioneered a neutron transport tomography technique to determine flow regimes and fractions in fluid flowing infuel channels.

General Management/Operations Management

- As a senior member of the plant engineering layout team responsible for facility efficiency, was able to improve production capability by 300% over a one year period.
- Conducted an individual store needs assessment and using this information as a base, designed, developed and implemented a model for an appliance stock program resulting in the provision all western stores with the appropriate, workable product for their trading needs.
- Conducted organizational assessments identifying operational issues and initiatives for improvement resulting in increased efficiency, improved customer service and improved gross sales.
- Developed and implemented revised operating methodologies resulting in productivity improvements up to 100% and individual cost reductions ranging to $1 million.
- Devised, developed and implemented corporate 1, 5 and 15 year operating plans.
- Implemented an audit system to identify incorrect freight rates, recovering substantial dollars and avoiding future overpayment and loss of interest.
- Instrumental in start-up phase of a new $20 million corporation through establishing and implementing administrative procedures, hiring and training staff, co-ordinating all travel, negotiating corporate rates, promoting display facility through effective use of print and electronic media, writing and designing corporate information sheets and brochures as well as establishing an executive level administrative and logistical service to a 21-person Board of Directors.
- Led and managed a national business unit with a multi-million dollar operating budget. Maintained the highest client retention rate in the industry. Continually met or exceeded budgeted profitability.
- Maximized safety by introducing new policies, procedures and equipment resulting in decreased accident frequency and personnel lost time.

Health Care Management

- As an independent contractor, conducted research on pallative care services resulting in the development of a major report and recommendations.
- As weekend senior nurse for a large national health care agency, supervised staff who conducted over 400 scheduled daily visits in the community.
- Co-authored a "Joint Program Protocol" with a major university.

Provided leadership to implement the protocol through the development of joint programs in nursing and child care.

- Developed, designed, tested and applied a community based, health promotion and wellness assessment tool to be used as an initial patient intervention strategy.
- Established a system and procedure for the implementation of workplace health and safety standards.
- For a major university, co-ordinated a community based practicum program for students in nursing, pharmacy and dental hygiene providing orientation, clinical instruction and follow-up.
- Managed and supervised the provision of patient care in a clinical setting with a total departmental budget of $800,000.
- Over a 20-year period, managed and supervised the nursing staff of 30-bed department in a large city facility.
- Participated in value improvement programs that resulted in the change of healthcare practice and an annual cost saving.
- Successfully collaborated with a national nursing service and a professional association to implement a first of its kind health care program with a primary focus on education.

Hospitality Management

- Successfully operated and managed a two location franchise delicatessen type of restaurant. Developed the business and was responsible for financial accountability, sales, purchasing, inventory control, staffing and customer relations.
- Conducted an organizational assessment, identified operational issues and designed a strategic plan for improvements which resulted in increased profitability by $7 million over a one-year timeframe.
- Launched and successfully led multi-million dollar renovations and hotel expansion projects which included food/beverage facilities, beach and public areas, in Australia, Canada and the United Kingdom. Results in consistent sales and profit increases.
- Established effective control systems, reduced food/beverage costs, utility and administration costs while increasing efficiency and productivity.
- Streamlined operations, improved employee relations and eliminated waste resulting in increased profitability over a six month time frame.

- Through consistent staff training, motivation and evaluation programs, successfully maintained high standards in a variety of hospital settings ranging from hotels, resorts, casinos and private clubs.
- Initiated, co-ordinated and directed very successful and profitable national and international conferences and special events and extended full service hospitality products to as many as 10,000 delegates.
- Demonstrated quick, calm, proactive abilities during a major disaster and rescue operation resulting in recovered sales profits by maintaining extraordinary guest and staff relations.

Human Resources

- Conducted a job analysis of the staff sales position. Based on this, developed an orientation program for all new staff inclusive of administrative procedures, key product knowledge and critical selling points.
- Designed national organizational structure, defined and wrote specific job descriptions, developed and implemented leading industry compensation package. Subsequent staff retention rates became industry standard.
- Developed and implemented policy manuals, which included job descriptions, employee orientation and performance evaluation programs. Resulted in improved morale and a commitment to service excellence.
- Developed an organizational policy manual which included job descriptions, customer sales requirements, credit limits, nature of business transactions, work schedules, dress code, employee skill requirements and training reimbursement program.
- Managed the co-ordination and implementation of changes to the handling of insurance disability claims. Designed new reporting forms resulting in more efficient processing.
- Managed a 130 volunteer program which included planning selection, supervision and replacement and planning resulting in an overall contribution to the success of the Western Canada Games.
- Managed the co-ordination and implementation of operational changes to assimilate large operations, administration, human resources development and culture change following merger of two multi-million dollar businesses.

- Over a ten year period, successfully supervised and managed a diverse professional and non professional staff of 60, scheduled at approximately 20 per shift on a 24 hour basis. Maintained a stable workforce in a difficult social service environment.
- Structured staff assignments to incorporate individual strengths and weaknesses resulting in improved customer satisfaction through reduced response time, call duration and increased employee productivity.

Manufacturing

- Acted as a key team member in the construction of a new multi-million dollar high technology facility. Computerization of the production system significantly reduced labour requirements.
- As Plant Supervisor, recorded a 20% annual increase in a 95,000 square foot ageing plant.
- Co-ordinated the transfer of a manufacturing and industrial support centre to a new location. This included thousands of items of manufacturing tooling for over 120 product line items as well as technical publications and documentation.
- Conducted an assessment of maintenance downtime; developed a human resources plan which required skilled millwrights to maintain equipment. Downtime was reduced substantially within a three year period.
- Designed, developed and implemented an Equipment Condition and Operating Security Audit Sheet to be utilized for evaluating machinery, buildings and equipment and estimating equipment replacement cost.
- Designed and supervised the manufacturing of several pieces of equipment including a cabling machine, vacuum loading equipment, dies and various machine components.
- Established emergency policies and procedures for fire protection, electrical, fuel and vital services including fire fighting procedures, plans of action, co-ordination of plans, salvage procedures and contingency plans.
- Initiated, co-ordinated and managed an industrial hygiene program including assessments and remediation programs for noise control, crystalline silica exposure, pulmonary function, WHMIS, asbestos, lead, radiation, hearing, soil, P.C.B.'s and environmental workplace safety.
- Researched, designed, developed and implemented an innovative production process and blending formula to increase product yield and plant efficiency.

- Researched and designed new breakthrough, batch processing tanks with specialized liners to withstand abrasion and corrosion. Resulted in major cost savings as well as meeting future health codes.

Marketing

- Co-created and launched a successful marketing program that has since been adopted by all national competitor agencies as a key component to major fall product launch programs.
- Co-ordinated cross promotional informational brochures and programs such as a discount card program which resulted in a substantial increase in consumer response.
- Designed and implemented a strong marketing strategy which within the first year, resulted in the turnaround of a three-year company sales decline.
- Designed, implemented and supervised five domestic and imported product lines while consistently meeting annual company objectives.
- Developed and implemented an effective merchandising and marketing program for two major accounts with a combined retail base of 90 stores.
- Designed, developed and consulted on the implementation of private label programs for several national retail clients.
- Identified market niches for new products and services in the environmental field and developed and implemented a program which surpassed first year target goals.
- Played a role as part of a national senior management committee. Redefined the organizational structure, developed, directed and implemented national operations, annual marketing programs to support $120 million in sales, and national employee incentive and development programs.

Negotiation

- Formulated a strategy for negotiation of a $50 million per year energy supply contract. Analyzed significantly complex costing and pricing arrangement and negotiated a savings of $750,000 and capital savings of $4 million.
- Negotiated and administered all contracts pertinent to new office premises, the relocation and operational recovery of a ten-person team. Project was conducted on time and on budget.
- Negotiated and administered all leasing and financing contracts for the purchase of equipment ranging from facsimile machines to heavy equipment, computer systems and aircraft.

- Negotiated the rights to use research data developed for a project fully paid by a client at no extra cost to the company.
- Planned, organized and controlled the negotiation of three divisional distribution systems into a single efficient responsive system.
- Successfully conducted meetings with highly technical and diversified clients to develop an environment of mutual confidence for negotiating and securing multi-million dollar contract sales.
- Initiated and successfully negotiated a strategic alliance with a main supplier resulting in a mutually beneficial arrangement and significant corporate cost reductions.
- Led and negotiated all transitional corporate, financial and organizational aspects of several major business acquisitions.
- Negotiated a significant financial package to provide for business acquisitions of a multi-million dollar corporation.
- Successfully utilized negotiation skills to achieve cost savings, profit realizations and good long term relationships with vendors and external commercial clients.

Non-profit Management/Government Relations

- As Chairperson of a 37-member federal government committee, for 2.5 years, planned all conferences, seminars and related special events.
- Assumed a major and leading role in a consulting team engaged to provide interim management in a major government services organization in a period of major change.
- Chaired a Board of Directors of a non-profit community nursery school which operated at a lower cost than the provincially funded allocations.
- Co-ordinated, administered, monitored and promoted a pilot project for a curbside multi-material waste reduction program answerable to three levels of government and a Board of Directors.
- Communicated effectively and diplomatically with professional colleagues and subordinates as an analyst and a director, as an intermediary for the executive, and as an advisor to boards and senior political officials.
- Co-ordinated both experienced and inexperienced volunteers in the development of a live stage festival in a series of different venues delivered simultaneously. Involved in the advertising, promotion, ticket control and scheduling for all events.

- Developed strategic and operational plans, policies and procedures for the leadership and management of an organizational unit consisting of 40 departments, a staff complement of 535 and an enrollment of 4,000 full-time and 19,000 continuing education students.
- Enhanced institutional profile and recognition by ensuring the increase of accredited programs. Provided executive support for the achievement of national or provincial accreditation of 16 programs over a seven year time period.
- In the role of Corporate Secretary and Acting Vice President – Finance, developed a budget under severe time and financial constraints, and recommended reorganization to several major areas of a large crown corporation.

Project Management

- Custom designed and project managed the installation of the first wheelchair accessible play structure in the city.
- Designed and co-ordinated a $200,000 renovation resulting in expanded capabilities and improved sales of 25%.
- Established objectives for project management including planning, VIP services, volunteerism and standards for success.
- Facilitated and co-ordinated the custom design and construction of the first water play structure for an existing city park wading pool.
- Led and conducted an organizational analysis and restructured the organization, resulting in the reduction of overhead costs by an average of 20% while increasing revenue by 30%.
- Spearheaded and led the planning and implementation of renovation projects and equipment/staff relocation. Ensured effective use of limited space and storage with minimal disruption resulting in prevention of total closure of services and loss of revenue.
- Supervised the progress of seven project teams, ensuring that all tasks were completed on time and management was continuously informed of progress and approved adjustments when necessary.

Policy Development/Management

- Appointed by the corporate President to serve on a task force to develop policies and a five year plan resulting in improved quality of programming.
- As a member of a team, researched changes to the Federal Government Operational Planning Framework. Developed a Funding Analysis worksheet to be completed by grant recipients which assisted in the identification of financial mismanagement.
- Conceptualized, proposed and co-ordinated the development and delivery of the new provincial policy which accredits experiential training.
- Developed and implemented the record management policy and trained all staff on procedures enabling a government department to conform with the Freedom of Information Act within the required implementation timeframe.
- Developed, documented and implemented policies in key operational areas such as personnel, investment administration and board relations and protocol.
- Designed and managed a specialized corporations creditors arrangement act reorganization.
- Devised and directed over 100 research studies which analyzed the application and interpretation of numerous federal and provincial statutes, policies, procedures and practices in areas such as taxation, employment equity, accreditation, broadcasting and race relations.
- Developed a program evaluation model and supportive policies which were flexible, accountable and involved all program stakeholders. The process and its results have received recognition provincially and nationally.
- Established policies and standards for project management including planning, VIP services, and volunteer workforce.
- Participative management style implemented policies and procedures for ensuring excellence and integrity in customer relations and service.
- Researched and analyzed government regulations in order to formulate plant policies and procedures to effectively operate within new environmental regulations.

Public Relations/Events Planning

- Created and implemented strategic communication packages including event planning, media relations and collateral materials development for public and private enterprises.
- Created, promoted and sold seniors matinees. This required extensive organization, scheduling, advertising, direct sales and the management of transportation issues.
- Developed a newsletter as a means of communicating with and improving retention of employees for an internal department. This served to be a key tool to develop departmental and individual recognition, share product knowledge and build a cohesive team.
- Devised and instituted various town hall sessions and scholar-in-residence programs resulting in the attraction of international speakers and presenters and capacity audiences.
- For a provincial government department, co-ordinated communications activities, managed a resource centre and consistently completed projects within predetermined timeframes and budgets, while meeting stringent standards.
- For diverse client groups, prepared attractively presented public education/communication materials which focused on numerous issues of current concern in a variety of disciplines.
- Launched a successful public relations and fund-raising venture which promoted programs and services resulting in increased commitment and overall financial support.
- Led and successfully co-ordinated all requirements of a five day international conference hosting delegates from 86 countries.
- Organized and co-ordinated logistics for public meetings and events including a highly successful rally for seniors that was instrumental in forcing a reversal in federal government policy.
- Planned and co-ordinated a four day national conference. Required daily interaction with member agencies, international counterparts and government representatives. Prepared conference budget and funding applications and maintained accounts relating to conference.
- Successfully developed good public relations with community agencies and networks, giving acknowledgement and praise for liaison abilities from them.

Retail Sales And Marketing Management

- As regional manager, supervised and worked in conjunction with store managers to oversee and ensure the efficient functioning of retail stores. Volume sales increased by 50% in twelve months. Successfully maintained customer satisfaction and service.
- Contributed $1.5 million of profit in two combined territories by building and maintaining the highest profit margin within the corporate group while operating in a very aggressive competitive market.
- Created innovative field system tools which saved time, and increased planning and target setting efficiency. This included electronic data equipment and user friendly territory call schedules, field reports and easy professional sales techniques and selling formats.
- Developed and implemented integrated distributor, agent and key account market plans, thereby aligning price strategies and mutual marketing efforts, resulting in greatly improved communications.
- Developed an innovative marketing plan which increased sales by 220% over six years, and increased market share by 50% during a time of high competition in an industry dominated by four companies.
- Focused the company's market presence and improved customer service through the implementation of a regional toll-free line, increased regional advertising and the establishment and implementation of single desk ordering.
- Identified a former representative's move to a competitor, performed a successful search for a replacement, re-established direct account contact, developed and tracked intelligency and retained $1.0 million sales in a large provincial territory.
- Transformed departmental operating expenses to become largely proportionate to sales performance, thereby protecting corporate vulnerability in difficult economic times and at the same time contributed more than $250,000 of previous annual expense to bottom line profit through an innovative sales approach.
- Utilized a creative and highly leveraged sales approach through special events and 13 mass repeat print media to establish a highly recognized and leading volume operations.

Social Services Management

- Advocated for children with misunderstood and neglected needs. Investigated and determined relationships between children, parents and social workers.
- Analyzed the social and financial effects of a public housing rent scale on over 2,000 families in seven communities. Used the results to design, develop and present a revised system which was later accepted and implemented by the communities.
- Developed and implemented the computerized Fine Option and Community Service programs currently used by offenders who are unable to pay their fines.
- In order to deal with the results of service cutbacks to client capacity, designed and implemented a quota list system enabling all agencies to priorize their facility usage.
- Played a key role in resolving personal crises and helping individuals regain control over difficult personal situations.

Technology/New Ventures

- Participated as a key team member in the technical investigation of recurring compressor stalls for a gas turbine engine. The result was a reduction in the rate of stall occurrence. Investigations were conducted for hydraulic system anomalies and mechanical malfunctions with successful results.
- Founded, owned and operated a dealership for several well known large equipment manufacturers. Developed the business from a corner service station to the areas' largest dealership with the most advanced repair and service facility.
- Co-founded a specialized sheet metal fabrication and heli-arc welding company which following the establishment of a diversified product line. The company grew from three to one hundred employees and sales of over $6 million in 10 years.
- Founded and owner/managed a new venture in the airline business which was eventually developed into a three-tier marketing business including retail, wholesale and mail-order.
- Researched and formed a new company which offered communication services between aboriginal and non-aboriginal business, markets and cultures.

Training And Development

- Acted as a facilitator at conferences and designed and or delivered training courses on such diverse subjects as sexual harassment, telephone systems, effects of technology on the work place, interview techniques and assertiveness training.
- Conducted and moderated confidential customer focus group meetings. Managed a project in conjunction with the university marketing faculty to develop, distribute and analyze a customer survey to learn more about client expectations.
- Co-designed and delivered three programs over a ten month timeframe, requiring a diverse range of knowledge and skill development objectives. Created trainer and trainee manuals and conducted an evaluation of each program.
- In a variety of subject areas, conceived, developed, wrote and published staff training programs; selected and incorporated complementary audio-visual materials which introduced new concepts, increased program and policy knowledge and resulted in the increase of employee productivity.
- Facilitated workshops at both the provincial and national levels on a variety of subjects ranging from small business management to child care.
- Designed, developed, co-ordinated and delivered a six week experiential college credit program delivered in Europe.
- Organized and developed individual and group training sessions about the use of databases in various formats, including CD-ROM and Internet, with consistently positive feedback.
- Pioneered a stand alone word processing instructional package and successfully introduced the program on a national basis.
- Recruited and trained specialized staff for a community supplementary school and youth program.
- Researched, designed and delivered office skills programs in both French and English.

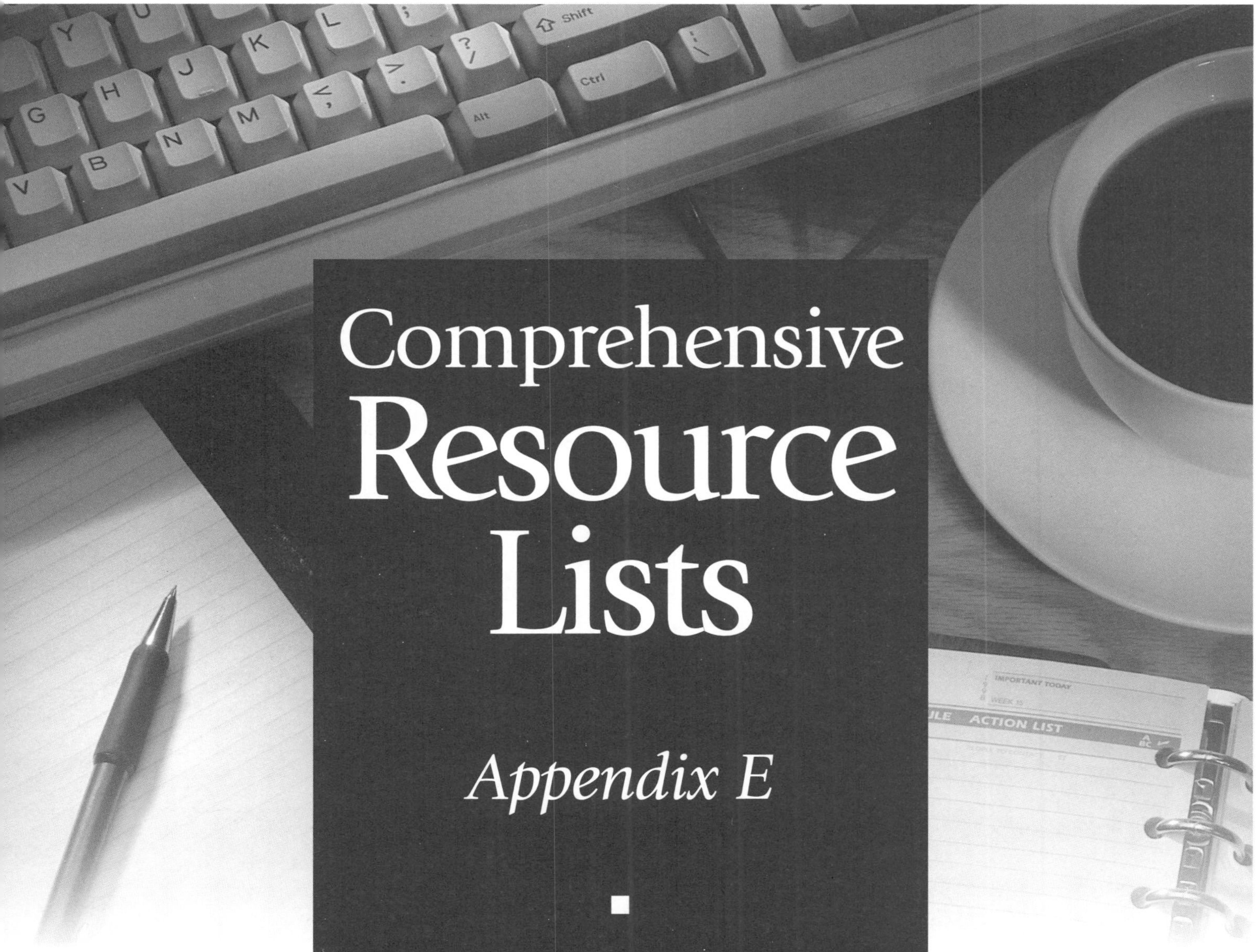

Comprehensive Resource Lists

Appendix E

■

Selected

Résumé

Samples

Selected Résumé Samples

A select number of résumés are provided for you to demonstrate that the transferable résumé style can be applied to most professions. Note that page one of each résumé is similar but that the following pages and sections are then customized to meet the need of the individual writer.

BARBARA J. BOWES

48 Résumé Drive
Winnipeg, Manitoba
ROX 3B6

A chartered accountant with over 10 years' experience as controller, manager and financial consultant to businesses in the public and private sectors. Highly motivated and innovative with exceptional skills in analyzing, developing and implementing computer systems. Seeking an opportunity that welcomes a strong work ethic and commitment to corporate goals.

PROFESSIONAL EXPERTISE

- Extensive experience in the preparation and analysis of monthly and year end financial statements, annual budgets, quarterly forecasts, cash flow projections and capital requirements.
- Demonstrated bottom line accomplishments through solid supervision and management of financial reporting and control functions in a multi-million dollar operating environment.
- Excellent strengths in computer-assisted financial planning, analysis and the design of customized spreadsheets in the areas of profit plan development, capital plans, cost analysis, and financial statement preparation.
- Well developed skills in capital resource investment, audit and evaluation with experience in the development of replacement and preventative maintenance programs.
- Solid interpersonal and human resource management strengths with the capacity to work with a variety of people in a dynamic, supportive and participative work environment.
- Good oral and written communication skills; able to provide well thought out summaries and reports that are easily understood and logically presented.

ACCOMPLISHMENTS

- Administered an annual budget of $30.5 million, achieving budgetary surpluses each year while also significantly expanding business.
- Co-ordinated the computer implementation for the financial reporting and management of information requirements for six national corporate subsidiaries.
- Designed, developed, negotiated and implemented an electronic payment system resulting in more efficient payment and improved company receivables.
- Pursuant to the sale of company to a large multinational, redesigned the management reporting, budgeting and financial statement presentations to comply with the new parent requirements.

EDUCATION/PROFESSIONAL DEVELOPMENT

Bachelor of Commerce, University of Northern Saskatchewan, 1982
Total Quality Management for Controllers,
Canadian Manufacturers Association and University of Alberta
Canadian Investment Finance, Canadian Securities Institute, Toronto
Creating a highly motivated finance team, Community College

WORK HISTORY

CONTROLLER, Canadian Express, Winnipeg, 1990–present
ASSISTANT CONTROLLER, Canadian Express, Winnipeg, 1988–1990
ASSISTANT CONTROLLER, St. James Cartage and Storage, 1985–1988

BARBARA J. BOWES

48 Résumé Drive
Winnipeg, Manitoba
ROX 3B6

Senior corporate finance executive with keen business acumen, extensive experience and expertise in strategic financial planning and reporting, treasury and banking, risk management, accounting, management information systems and human resource compensation and benefits. Strong negotiator and decision maker with excellent interpersonal and presentation skills; seeking executive career challenges in a sophisticated customer service and results-oriented environment.

PROFESSIONAL EXPERTISE

- Highly developed organizational, administrative and financial management strengths utilizing continuous quality improvement for the efficient and effective management of office structure, day-to-day operations including systematizing allocation of resources and monitoring workload.
- Corporate-level financial and economic analysis skills and experience in major acquisitions, divestitures and capital expenditure decisions.
- Excellent treasury and banking expertise including negotiating and structuring corporate credit, foreign exchange and interest rate risk management, cash flow management and related policy development.
- Exceptionally creative with substantial ability and success in the identification of customer and business trends, the identification and exploitation of market opportunities, conducting competitive analysis and the initiation and design of co-ventured partnerships.
- Demonstrated ability to develop staffing, compensation and benefit plans for the integration of human resources with other corporate business plans resulting in overall productivity improvements and cost reductions.

ACCOMPLISHMENTS

- Assumed the responsibilities of corporate controller for an extended period. Communicated with divisions and established report requirements, deadlines and issued monthly, quarterly financial statements, budgets and profit plans in a timely manner.

- Implemented a daily cash flow analysis allowing management to forecast monthly expenditures to minimize use of bank overdraft.
- Pursuant to the sale of the company to a large multinational, redesigned the management reporting, budgeting and financial statement presentations to comply with the new parent requirements.
- Prepared and maintained payroll records up to and including T-4 preparation. Designed, implemented and monitored cash and financial controls.
- Successfully established and implemented cost control systems resulting in a 15% profit increase.
- Under personal leadership, directly contributed to achieving record profit during a downturn in the economy.

PROFESSIONAL/COMMUNITY LEADERSHIP

Vice President, Finance Executives, Vancouver, 1994-current
Professional of the Year Award, National Association of Finance Executives, 1992
Chair, Discipline Committee, Finance Executives, Vancouver, 1990–1994
Chair, Professional Development Committee, Institute of Chartered Accountants, 1989 – 1990
Member, Professional Development/Examination Committees, Institute of Chartered Accountants, 1981 –1989
Guest Lecturer, Management Studies, University of British Columbia, 1981–current

EMPLOYMENT HISTORY

Chief Financial Officer, Cassan Corporation, Vancouver, 1990–1995
Assistant To the Chief Financial Officer, Cassan Corporation, 1985–1990
National Controller, Johnson Western Equipment Distributors, Vancouver, 1981–1985

EDUCATION

Business Administration (MBA), University of Manitoba, in progress
Chartered Accountant, Manitoba Institute of Chartered Master of Accountants, 1980
Master of Accounting, University of New York, 1978

BARBARA J. BOWES

48 Résumé Drive
Winnipeg, Manitoba
ROX 3B6

Enterprising, innovative communications and public relations professional with significant project management skills for the management of major communications campaigns in both the private and public sector. Exceptional team leadership, organizational and motivational skills for the achievement of clearly defined goals and measurable results. Seeking an opportunity to become a key contributor in a team-oriented environment.

PROFESSIONAL EXPERTISE

- Significant experience and expertise in all aspects of communications, public and media relations including television, radio and print media.
- Significant creativity for concept and implementation of unique and effective public relations and marketing strategies in multi-task, change oriented and time sensitive environments.
- Superior organizational expertise for project management of national and local events followed by the planning, co-ordination, implementation and follow through of strategies necessary for successful project completion.
- Detailed and results-oriented leadership drive complemented by a participative and flexible approach to team management.
- Excellent research strengths with skills in market trend analysis and the development of strategic plans to meet market needs.
- Outstanding presentation skills.
- Action-oriented innovator able to meet time and budget targets by strategic analysis of possibilities, employing logic and ingenuity.

ACHIEVEMENTS

- Supervised all stages of television commercial production for a large Western Canadian Corporation; co-ordinated and managed all efforts of advertising agencies and various production house resources.
- Managed the input of freelance resources in the development of marketing communications and advertising projects including graphic designers, printers, photographers, and audio and video production specialists.
- Created and implemented strategic communication packages including event planning, media relations and collateral materials development for public and private enterprise.
- Organized and coordinated logistics for public meetings and events including a highly successful rally for seniors that was instrumental in forcing a reversal in government policy.
- Facilitated communication and provided objective leadership between government, community, business and labour groups.

WORK HISTORY

WRITER/PRODUCER, Dow and Dow Advertising, Winnipeg, 1990–1995
CREATIVE SUPERVISOR, Carlton/Hall Productions, Toronto, 1980–1990
CREATIVE DIRECTOR, PRINT, Mint and Burkley Marketing, Toronto
MANAGER OF COMMUNICATIONS AND PROTOCOL, Backfield Corporation

EDUCATION/PROFESSIONAL DEVELOPMENT

Applied Arts Diploma – Creative Communications, Local Community College, 1980
Report and Letter Writing
MacIntosh Levels 1,2,3

BARBARA J. BOWES

48 Résumé Drive
Winnipeg, Manitoba
ROX 3B6

Highly motivated, results-oriented and experienced information systems professional with extensive expertise in designing, developing and managing information technology networks, systems and services. A strategic planner who balances future possibilities, resource restraints and current mission into socio-technological designs.

PROFESSIONAL EXPERTISE

- Excellent analytical strengths for complex organizational and problem analysis, productivity and quality improvement analysis, work simplification, job analysis and major systems design.
- Computer strengths in both mainframe and personal computing utilizing spreadsheets, word processing, and automated office, including local and wide area networking.
- Broad knowledge and experience in matching appropriate technologies, designs and systems development techniques with an organization's needs, capabilities and resources.
- Excellent ability to communicate technical information and possibilities to team members, peers, management and clients, and to provide written reports that are easily understood and logically presented.
- Action-oriented innovator who is able to meet time and budget targets by strategic planning.
- Effective human resources and leadership skills for the development and fostering of a successful teamwork environment resulting in timely project management.
- Good training capabilities with experience in training both users and management in new programs and computerized software.
- Computer expertise includes: MVS, JCL, TSO, UNIX, MPE, VMS,DCL,RDB, Word ll, 20/20, DOS, Windows, OS2, dBase, Paradox, Oracle, TimeLine, Excel, Quattro, 1–2–3, Word for Windows, WordPerfect, Novell Netware, DECnet, Adabas/Natural, Oracle, Paradox, C, Cobol, PL1, Fortran, Basic, Powerhouse, SPSS, SAS.

ACCOMPLISHMENTS

- Acted as lead consultant to convert a mainframe MIS to a client/server LAN architecture; negotiated, presented, implemented, converted, enhanced and integrated the systems plus developed the procedures, programs and controls to interconnect with external systems.

- Developed and implemented a computer strategy for a large government agency with the end result being the installation of a computer room, tendering and implementation of a VAX 6210 in the head office and 5 VAX 3300's in the regional offices. Each office was networked to the head office.
- Developed and implemented a record management policy and procedure for a government department to conform with the Freedom of Information Act, with the result being that reports were produced on a timely basis and staff were trained in procedures.
- Developed and implemented the computerized Fine Option and Community Service Order Program which is now being utilized across Canada for offenders who are unable to pay their fines.
- Supervised the progress of seven project teams and ensured that all tasks were completed on time.
- Initiated a LAN of UNIX and PC workstations with gateway to remote IBM mainframe – raising productivity by 17%.
- Developed an innovative Research Costing System to improve transfer pricing and controls plus a satellite fed database system while concurrently managing other small department projects.

PROFESSIONAL WORK HISTORY

MIS CONSULTANT, ACE Computer Technology, 1994–present
DIRECTOR, INFORMATION SYSTEMS, National School Academy, 1986–1994
INFORMATION ANALYST, Oil Research Resource Centre, 1981–1986
SENIOR SYSTEMS ANALYST, Government of Alberta
REGIONAL SYSTEMS CO-ORDINATOR, Government of Ontario

PROFESSIONAL DEVELOPMENT/EDUCATION

Certificate, Applied Artificial Intelligence
Certificate, Telecommunications, Communications Institute
Certificate, Logical Data Analysis, Locale Community College

Office Automation
DEC VAX/VMS Systems Performance Management
EDP Security Assurance Review and Risk Analysis
EDP Auditing Tools and Techniques
Network Management 1

BARBARA J. BOWES, P.Eng
48 Résumé Drive
Winnipeg, Manitoba
ROX 3B6

A professional engineer with over twenty years' experience and extensive management expertise in diverse manufacturing and operating environments. Demonstrated proficiency in the integration of people and resources to maximize productivity and increase production.

PROFESSIONAL EXPERTISE

- Strong organizational and administrative strengths for the development and implementation of operating and financial work plans.
- Demonstrated expertise in human resources management complemented by well developed interpersonal skills and a proven track record in the establishment of positive working relations with all levels of personnel.
- Creative approach to problem solving with the ability to view a problem from several perspectives, develop alternative solutions and recommend appropriate resolution.
- Extensive experience in the evaluation, selection, installation and commissioning of a wide variety of manufacturing equipment in diverse environments.
- Excellent project management skills with significant expertise in the management of diverse projects including identification of issues, planning, budgeting, implementation and monitoring for successful completion.
- Assertive and effective communication style; able to provide written and verbal summaries and reports that are easily understood and logically presented.
- Solid understanding of environmental assessment procedures with ability to manage the corporate requirements of a licensing process.

ACCOMPLISHMENTS

- For over 15 years, successfully managed plant profit responsibility for a $45 million Canadian division of a multi-product international corporation. Managed 125 employees and oversaw all functional areas of operation including human resources management, sales, marketing, manufacturing, distribution, and cost control.
- Developed, implemented and led a Total Quality Management program resulting in an effective customer-oriented organization, which acted as the model for the parent organization.
- Improved inventory control systems resulting in improved customer service through reduced back orders and reduced costs. Improved purchasing practises, shipping/receiving controls and overall inventory turnover.
- Expanded production capabilities to match 300% sales growth while at the same time reducing unit product costs.

EMPLOYMENT HISTORY

PLANT MANAGER, Dominion Electronics, Montreal, 1980–1995
GENERAL MANAGER, Canadian Liquids Manufacturing, 1971–1980

PROFESSIONAL DEVELOPMENT/EDUCATION

Certificate in Management (CIM), Canadian Institute of Management, 1974
Effective Supervision, Montreal Institute of Management
Frontline Leadership, Zenger-Miller
Workplace Health and Safety, Quebec Labour Council
Effective Interpersonal Skills, Xerox Learning Systems

BACHELOR OF COMMERCE (Honours), Concordia University
BACHELOR OF ARTS (Business Administration), Quebec College

BARBARA J. BOWES

48 Résumé Drive
Winnipeg, Manitoba
ROX 3B6

Results-oriented General Manager who thrives on the challenge of continuous improvement in a customer service environment. Proven skills in project management, training, recruitment and communication. Demonstrated expertise in operations analysis, systems development, loss prevention and risk management. Dedicated to maintaining and improving customer service without compromising profitability within a foods service environment.

PROFESSIONAL EXPERTISE

- Well developed customer service philosophy with proven skills in the development of award-winning service standards.
- Highly skilled in detailed and comprehensive analysis of financial information, inventory systems, training procedures and food preparation procedures.
- Demonstrated expertise in financial management and cost containment including budget determination and attainment, payroll procedures and controls, profit and loss analysis and waste minimization procedures.
- Human resource management skills including recruiting, employee training and development, performance appraisal procedures and employee relations.
- Strong organizational abilities for the development, implementation, co-ordination and management of business plans, marketing strategies, operational procedures and standards.
- Established proficiency in utilizing computer technology for the effective management of records, sales and costs.
- Participative management style with proven team building accomplishments to achieve desired goals.
- Strong interpersonal skills with a demonstrated ability for effective communications.

ACCOMPLISHMENTS

- Key member in the co-ordination of a new facility opening which achieved the lowest problem ratio of new openings for the restaurant chain.
- Redesigned a labour scheduling system to optimize labour hour apportionment. Increased service standards with no increase in operating costs.
- Following a detailed work analysis of time and employee allocation, instituted a strategy which reduced labour overtime 84% while maintaining customer service excellence.
- Designed and implemented management and employee training programs resulting in a hospitality award as well as an improvement of comprehension, knowledge, training consistency and overall employee satisfaction.
- Responsible for the management, training, development and co-ordination of a five person management team and a staff of 100 employees.
- Successfully operated a 250 seat, full service restaurant with consistently high achievement ratings for service, cleanliness, procedural integrity and guest service as determined by the corporate audit division.
- Conducted a review of facility maintenance costs, re-organized and restructured procedures and contractors, resulting in a savings of $20,000 within a twelve month period.

WORK HISTORY

GENERAL MANAGER, Carlton Gardens Restaurants (Manitoba), 1988–1994
UNIT MANAGER, Emma's Restaurants of Canada, 1980–1988
ASSISTANT MANAGER, Don's Pizza Palace

PROFESSIONAL DEVELOPMENT/EDUCATION

Management Development Program, Carlton Gardens Restaurants
Advanced Leadership Skills, Leadership Institute of Manitoba
Inventory Management, Leadership Institute of Manitoba
Advanced Micro-Computers, Harvard Community College

Certified General Accountant
Bachelor of Arts, Geography

BARBARA J. BOWES, C.I.M.

48 Résumé Drive
Winnipeg, Manitoba
ROX 3B6

Proven administrator and manager with excellent interpersonal and communication skills. A strong organizer and planner who is creative, innovative and entrepreneurial. Dedicated professional who thrives on challenge, possesses integrity and demonstrates initiative, professionalism and a positive attitude.

PROFESSIONAL EXPERTISE

- Well developed strategic business planning, financial management and operational skills with proven expertise and accomplishments in the co-ordination and management of complex, multi–site businesses.
- Superior negotiation skills for the achievement of cost savings, profit targets, and contracts.
- Participative management style with proven team building accomplishments complemented by excellent interpersonal skills resulting in the achievement of desired goals.
- Demonstrated success at setting objectives and achieving goals within a challenging, fast-paced environment.
- Experienced in human resources management including employee selection, evaluation, supervision and development.
- Excellent written and oral communication strengths; able to write clear and concise technical and management reports and make presentations.
- Solid customer service philosophy with a focus on customer satisfaction and the development of long term relationships with customers and suppliers.

ACCOMPLISHMENTS

- Undertook strategic planning, as well as led a major corporate downsizing of a multi-site operation resulting in the seamless facilitation of layoffs and terminations
- Designed, developed and implemented a new organizational structure which resulted in the improvement of operation and efficiency.
- Strategized and negotiated a strategic alliance with a competitor resulting in the collaboration of a new and highly successful corporate venture with the partnership continuing today.
- Using customer service expertise complemented by negotiation and communication strengths, was able to secure a large corporate client from a previously long term competitive relationship.

WORK HISTORY

GENERAL MANAGER, Versity Batteries, Slokan, Ontario, 1983–1995
ASSISTANT GENERAL MANAGER, Halcyon Turbo and Fuel, Downsview, Ont., 1977–1983
BRANCH MANAGER, Reno Equipment, Arnsworth, Ontario, 1966–1977

EDUCATION

Certificate in Management, Rowland Community College, Downsview
Total Quality Management, Rowland Community College, Downsview
Effective Speaking, Dale Carnegie

BARBARA J. BOWES, Ph.D., M.S.W.
48 Résumé Drive
Winnipeg, Manitoba
ROX 3B6

Experienced, professional manager specializing in the health/service sector. Committed to integrity, pursuing a vision focusing on solutions and turning complex problems into opportunities. Strong analytical problem solving, negotiation and decision making skills with extensive Canadian and International experience in Health and Rehabilitation. Seeking highly responsible management challenges.

PROFESSIONAL EXPERIENCE

- Exceptional skills and innate ability to effectively lead and motivate professional staff towards a mission which targets organizational needs and produces significant positive change over time.
- High level of expertise in program planning, needs assessments, implementation design, delivery and evaluation.
- Experience in research, needs assessment and evaluation design, proposal writing, survey design, implementation, data analysis and report writing.
- Broad human resource expertise and experience including recruitment, selection, organizational audits, program evaluation, policy development and review.
- Strong interpersonal and negotiation skills, effective communication to all levels including senior managers, government, volunteer boards and executive, consignors and colleagues. Equality strong in oral and written modes of communication.
- Solid foundation and working knowledge of health, rehabilitation and disability issues, DSM 111, child welfare, employment equity and vocational rehabilitation.

MAJOR ACCOMPLISHMENTS

- Initiated needs assessments and feasibility studies and negotiated funds for local interest groups resulting in three community-based resource centres which have sustained and expanded over the past decade.
- Directed a research team to implement a needs assessment of a professional organization resulting in a 90% membership return rate.

- Directed a management team to implement a marketing strategy which resulted in a 50% increase in community inclusion activities within a four month period.
- Designed, implemented and managed group training programs which have served as models within the disabled community locally, nationally and internationally.
- Researched, developed, implemented and evaluated five pilot curriculum programs, supervised the revisions with the result that the programs were successfully implemented on an international basis.
- Planned and implemented a highly interactive workshop to prepare professional personnel in a series of new client intervention techniques which resulted in a 75% decline in worker injury.

EMPLOYMENT HISTORY

Curriculum Consultant, ATCC Human Services Agency, Winterton, British Columbia, 1991–1993

Adjunct Faculty, Mount Mantee College, North Dakota, Thinker Hari Prasaad College, India, University of Winterton, Garden Grove College, 1988–1991

Program Manager/Vocational Rehab Counsellor, Vocational Rehabilitation Services, Province of Saskatchewan, Saskatoon, 1979–1988

EDUCATION/PROFESSIONAL DEVELOPMENT

Ph.D., Community Health, University of British Columbia, 1991

M.S.W., Policy and Administration, University of Manitoba, 1985

Certificate, Rehabilitation Counselling, Manitoba, 1984

B.S.W., Industrial Social Work, University of Manitoba, 1978

Assorted skill development courses including *Non Violent Crisis Management, Stress Management, CPR, First Aid, Adult Learning Principles, Research Methodologies, Supervisory Skills and Time Management*

PROFESSIONAL AND COMMUNITY LEADERSHIP

Secretary Treasurer, National Society for Health Curriculum Manitoba Region, 1990-present

Member, Social Planning Council, Winterton, Man. 1988–present

Director, Canadian Association of Social Workers, Winterton Chapter, 1986–88

BARBARA J. BOWES

48 Résumé Drive
Winnipeg, Manitoba
ROX 3B6

Achievement driven marketing specialist with significant market planning skills, resourceful problem solving expertise and a proven track record. Creative, broad scope strategic thinker with strong presence and keen abilities in trend analysis, customer needs identification and marketing program development. Seeking the challenge of a results-oriented environment.

PROFESSIONAL EXPERTISE

- Exceptionally creative with substantial ability and success in the identification of customer and business trends, the identification and exploitation of market opportunities, conducting competitive analysis and the initiation and design of coventure programming.
- Skilled in strategic planning for corporate marketing and sales programming, complemented by a strong personal customer service and customer satisfaction philosophy.
- Strong leadership and administrative strengths for multi-million dollar budgetary responsibilities and line staff management with excellent interpersonal and human resource management skills.
- Considerable strengths in effective human resource management, recruitment, selection, training, motivating and performance evaluation.
- Significant oral communication and presentation skills for direct sales solicitation, sales presentations and internal staff training and development.
- A proven track record of working with a variety of people in dynamic, supportive and participative work environments.

ACCOMPLISHMENTS

- Created and implemented a computerized territory account planning system which facilitated the tracking, analysis and planning of specific geographic market plans and in turn the annual market plan.
- Developed, launched, co-ordinated and implemented a loyalty rewards retail program, which resulted in a card member base of approximately 50,000 and a retail/wholesale associate group in excess of 100 businesses in both urban and rural areas.

- As one of five key members of a national senior management committee, redefined the organizational structure, developed, directed and implemented national sales operations, annual marketing programs to support $54 million in sales, national employee incentives and development programs.
- Identified an ex-agent's move to a competitor, performed a successful search for a replacement agent, re-established direct account contact, developed and tracked market intelligence and thereby retained $1 million sales within a specified territory.
- Regained previously lost business with three strategic target accounts through the initiation of a key account sales effort resulting in an sales increase of $500,000.
- Co-developed and successfully launched an airplane points program which leveraged the corporate credit card system. Program was applied nationally and has since been adopted by all national credit card companies.

EXPERIENCE

GENERAL MANAGER, Royalty Rewards Limited Partnerships, Winnipeg
REGIONAL SALES MANAGER, Reliance Lumber, Lawsdone, Manitoba
DISTRICT MANAGER, Canadian Express, Manitoba
SENIOR SALES SUPERVISOR, Commercial Sales Department, OilGas Ltd.

PROFESSIONAL DEVELOPMENT/EDUCATION

Business Management Forum, Federal Business Development Bank
Selling Methods and Strategies, Cornerstone Management
Presentation Skills, Local Community College
Small Business Development
The Performance Edge
Professional Selling Skills

Bachelor of Commerce, Marketing, University of Alberta

BARBARA J. BOWES

48 Résumé Drive
Winnipeg, Manitoba
ROX 3B6

Visionary materials management professional with a successful track record in high volume materials management. Efficient, results-oriented leader with strong human resources, financial and leadership skills. Seeking an opportunity to make a significant contribution in a fast paced challenging environment.

PROFESSIONAL SKILLS

- **Maintaining** a full set of financial records up to and including monthly and annual variance reports.
- **Evaluating** variance reports and making adjustments as required.
- **Preparing and analyzing** detailed feasibility studies and carrying out an action plan for project development.
- **Excellent interpersonal skills** to co-ordinate and participate in a team environment and achieve organizational goals.
- Effective **control**, policy development and evaluation of both perpetual and annual inventories.
- **Liaison** with all levels of management regarding policies, procedure and standards for the shipping and receiving of goods.
- **Win/win negotiation approach** for arriving at jointly agreed upon decision and bringing reconciliation to differing people both in a union and non union environment.
- **Keen insights** and ability to identify key problems and generate creative solutions.
- **Creative and innovative** in the delivery of professional development, and group facilitation processes.
- Excellent **Customer Services** skills for dealing with internal and external clients.

ACCOMPLISHMENTS

- Received, inventoried and annually supplied $25 million in medical-surgical supplies to over 50 satellite departments/agencies.
- Prepared, implemented and supervised a department operating budget of $1 million; oversaw staff of 30.
- Using total quality management principles, successfully reorganized and streamlined physical stock for faster access.
- Acted as a key team member in the computerization of a facility wide computerized inventory ordering system.

WORK HISTORY

ASSISTANT DIRECTOR, Supply Services, Mountain Health Centre, Orillia, 1989–1994
PURCHASING MANAGER, Parts Department, Kingston Transport, Orillia, 1982–1989
HEAD, STORES AND WAREHOUSING, Health and Welfare Canada
INVENTORY SUPERVISOR, Health and Welfare Canada

PROFESSIONAL DEVELOPMENT

Management programs: Extensive workshops and seminars in the areas of warehouse, supervisory, financial, material management as well as the transportation of dangerous goods, hazardous chemicals and WHMIS.

BARBARA J. BOWES

48 Résumé Drive
Winnipeg, Manitoba
ROX 3B6

Experienced project management and building planning professional possessing demonstrated organizational abilities. Proven skills in project co-ordination and crisis management. Accomplished in providing on time and on budget project completion. Self-motivated analytical thinker with strong communication skills.

PROFESSIONAL EXPERTISE

- Excellent organizational and administrative skills with the ability to follow through on assignments to defined parameters.
- Assertive and effective communication and interpersonal skills. Reputation for providing easily understood and logically presented summaries and reports.
- Strong technical knowledge with superior strengths in planning, design and construction, stressing attention to accuracy and detail.
- Demonstrated ability to work with clients and associates at all staffing levels with a solid focus on customer service.
- Participative management style with proven teambuilding accomplishments.
- Solid understanding of national, provincial and civic building codes with ability to work effectively with jurisdictional authorities.
- Proven marketing ability to promote general and technical product information to facilitate material selection and specification.

ACCOMPLISHMENT SUMMARY

- Successfully managed a diverse array of projects having varying degrees of complexity and size.
- Utilized professional project control methodology to ensure timely, efficient and economical work performance.
- Led and co-ordinated design and construction teams on high quality interior design -oriented projects. Achieved completion schedules well ahead of industry standards.
- Consistently provided leadership to ensure that project completions occurred on schedule by proactively solving delivery and installation problems.

EMPLOYMENT HISTORY

MANAGER, Architectural Team Inc., Winnipeg, 1987–1993
PROJECT CO-ORDINATOR, Ace Design and Development, 1986–1987
PROJECT MANAGER/ESTIMATOR, Dominion Construction Ltd.
CONSTRUCTION CO-ORDINATOR, McLeods Architectural Group

PROFESSIONAL DEVELOPMENT/EDUCATION

Certificate, Planning and Managing Working Drawings, University of Westgate
Certificate, Architectural Drawing, River Road College
Certificate, Computer Aided Drafting and Design, River Road Tech

Machine Drafting and Design, Westgage Technical School
Building Construction Technician, River Roach College

BARBARA J. BOWES

48 Résumé Drive
Winnipeg, Manitoba
ROX 3B6

A committed, versatile and innovative plant manager with over twenty years' experience in the management of manufacturing, sales, marketing and human resources. Demonstrated expertise in overall financial management, budget preparation and strategic planning, clearly focused on the bottom line.

PROFESSIONAL SKILLS

- A strong overall business background with a thorough understanding of all organizational functions and a demonstrated competence in managing them on a day-to-day basis.
- A positive, committed and adaptable management style that builds stability, loyalty and professional pride within the organization.
- Innovative and effective at improving production systems, work flow, productivity, product/service quality and individual/group performance.
- Accomplished human resource management strengths including recruitment, training, motivation, teambuilding and coaching.
- Talent for determining goals and objectives followed by the planning, organization, co-ordination and follow through necessary for successful project completion.
- Outstanding analytical abilities, able to package and communicate while still accounting for detail and inevitable exceptions.
- Experienced in policy and procedure formulation. Ability to plan, organize and follow through to implementation and control.
- Significant troubleshooting and crisis management skills; prepared to handle any given situation.

ACCOMPLISHMENTS

- For over 15 years, successfully managed plant profit responsibility for a $45 million Canadian division of a multi-product international corporation. Managed 125 employees and oversaw all functional areas of operation including human resources management, sales, marketing, manufacturing, distribution, and cost control.
- Developed, implemented and led a Total Quality Management program resulting in an effective customer-oriented organization, which acted as the model for the parent organization.
- Improved inventory control systems resulting in improved customer service through reduced back orders and reduced costs. Improved purchasing practises, shipping/receiving controls and overall inventory turnover.
- Expanded production capabilities to match 300% sales growth while at the same time reducing unit product costs.

EMPLOYMENT HISTORY

PLANT MANAGER, Dominion Electronics, Montreal, 1980–1995
GENERAL MANAGER, Canadian Liquids Manufacturing, 1971–1980

PROFESSIONAL DEVELOPMENT/EDUCATION

Certificate in Management (CIM), Canadian Institute of Management, 1974
Effective Supervision, Montreal Institute of Management
Frontline Leadership, Zenger-Miller
Workplace Health and Safety, Quebec Labour Council
Effective Interpersonal Skills, Xerox Learning Systems

BACHELOR OF COMMERCE (Honours), Concordia University
BACHELOR OF ARTS (Business Administration), Quebec College

BARBARA J. BOWES
48 Résumé Drive
Winnipeg, Manitoba
ROX 3B6

Innovative, proactive and dynamic health care professional skilled in communicating throughout the organization. Experienced professional manager specialising in program design, project management and organizational development. Looking for challenges utilizing skills to contribute to an organization.

PROFESSIONAL EXPERTISE

- Solid health care expertise for client health care assessments, and patient care education both within an institutional as well as an organizational work environment.
- Exceptional interpersonal and communication skills, sensitive to individual needs as they relate to group process and the goals of the organization.
- Skills in health program needs assessment, information analysis, program development, design and delivery at the patient and professional levels.
- Dynamic presentation style using innovative and proactive training methodologies and programs based on adult learning principles.
- Natural leader who can use persuasive communication to create win/win situations.
- Effective public relations skills with the ability to communicate concepts, and provide information at all organizational levels.
- Proficient at human resource and financial management in a multi-disciplinary work environment.

PROFESSIONAL ACHIEVEMENTS

- Led and managed a private sector health care personnel agency with a client base of over 250, and a staff resource of 50.
- Successfully collaborated with a non-profit health agency and a professional association to design and implement the first footcare program with a primary focus on prevention and health education.
- Designed, developed, pilot tested and applied a community based initial health assessment tool which was modelled on a health promotion and wellness structure.

- Co-ordinated a community-based practicum experience for over 50 university nursing, pharmacy and dental hygiene students providing orientation, clinical supervision and student follow-up.
- Gathered and analyzed data on Pallative Care services in three provinces; authored a report and presented a set of recommendations which have now been integrated into provincial policy in two out of the three provinces.
- Initiated and developed a strong participative team management approach while simultaneously facilitating the integration of a total quality management problem solving resulting in obtaining a three year Accreditation Certificate.
- Initiated and guided an issues-oriented Community Health Practice Program which brought about increased community awareness and involvement in home health care involvement.

EMPLOYMENT HISTORY

GENERAL MANAGER, Health by the Hour Services, Ottawa, Ont., 1981–1994
MANAGING DIRECTOR, Colburg Wellness Centre, Downsview, Ont., 1977–1981
CLINICAL INSTRUCTOR/STUDENT ADVISOR, University of Downsview, 1975–1977
PLANNING AND PROGRAM ANALYST, Province of Ontario
ASSISTANT DIRECTOR OF NURSING, St. Josephs on the Lake
CHARGE NURSE, Golden West Health Care Centre

EDUCATION/PROFESSIONAL DEVELOPMENT

MASTER OF BUSINESS ADMINISTRATION, University of St. John's, 1994
MASTER OF NURSING, University of North Dakota
BACHELOR OF NURSING, University of North Dakota

PROFESSIONAL/COMMUNITY LEADERSHIP

Invited Guest Speaker, Canadian Nursing Organizations, 1990–1994
Invited Guest Speaker/Lecturer, University of Downsview
Member, Local Association of Registered Nurses
Member, Quality Assurance Practitioners of Canada
Member, Health Education Practitioners of Canada
Director, Canadian Cancer Society

BARBARA J. BOWES

48 Résumé Drive
Winnipeg, Manitoba
ROX 3B6

An innovative, visionary leader with extensive experience with not-for-profit organizations. Highly organized with a proven track record of providing successful business direction and operation. Well developed expertise in strategic planning, financial management, organizational and staff development as well as marketing and fund-raising.

PROFESSIONAL EXPERTISE

- Solid knowledge of board managed organizations with the ability to develop strong professional relationships with board members and volunteers.
- Superior leadership, planning and administrative management skills for the day-to-day operations of a $10 million organization with up to 35 staff.
- Good working knowledge of financial and accounting principles with demonstrated expertise in long term financial planning, annual budgeting, monitoring and reporting.
- Good understanding of marketing and sales concepts as they apply to non-profit service programs; able to identify client needs and develop/refine programs to meet these needs.
- Excellent communication and public relations skills; proven success in the design, development and implementation of newsletters, program brochures.

ACCOMPLISHMENTS

- As a newly appointed Executive Director, conducted an organizational review and restructured the organization, thus improving the overall operation and efficiency.
- Facilitated and oversaw the design, development and implementation of polices in key operational areas such as personnel, administration, financial investments, board relations and board protocol.
- Led the task force on Total Quality management and applied procedures and tools to the organization resulting in seven teams in operation within one year and significant operating improvements.

- Conceptualized and authored a grants proposal which resulted in the largest grant received by the organization. Funds were used to completely computerize community service data requirements.
- Conceptualized and facilitated the development of a strategic alliance between my employer and a rival organization resulting in the provision of joint and complementary services to a major client.
- Designed and developed an informational pamphlet for public education with the goal to increase donation revenue. Donation revenue increased by 45% in the first year.

EMPLOYMENT HISTORY

EXECUTIVE DIRECTOR, British Columbia Cultural Centre, 1982–94
ASSISTANT EXECUTIVE DIRECTOR, Saskatchewan Historical Association, 1974–1981
PROGRAM MANAGEMENT SPECIALIST, Victoria Art History Centre

COMMUNITY/PROFESSIONAL LEADERSHIP

Chair, UNICEF, British Columbia, 1993–present
Chair, Fund-raising Committee, British Columbia, 1991–1993
Executive Co-Chair, Junior League of Victoria
Member, Board of Directors, Victoria Rehab Housing
Chair/Co-ordinator, Community Association of Food Banks
Exhibition Co-ordinator, Festival of Arts Communities

EDUCATION/PROFESSIONAL DEVELOPMENT

Marketing for Non-profit Associations, UBC
Accounting Systems for Non-profit Associations, UBC
Arts Policies and Institutions, British Council of the Arts
Problem Solving and Decision Making, Canadian Learning Systems

Diploma in Social Communications
Master of Art History

BARBARA J. BOWES, Ph.D., P.Eng.

48 Résumé Drive
Winnipeg, Manitoba
ROX 3B6

A research and development professional who possesses excellent expertise in several areas of mathematical and physical sciences. Significant experience in academic research with a specialization in the application of mathematical methods to industrial issues. High proficiency in R&D project management, rationalization, budget and proposal preparation, and technical liaison complemented by excellent interpersonal and organizational strengths.

PROFESSIONAL EXPERTISE

- Skilled in the ability to develop conceptual frameworks and theories for the assessment of scientific technical problems and situations on a practical level.
- Significant strengths in numerical methods research in a number of research areas including radioactive transfer, gas ignition and biomass systems, and fluid flow.
- Well developed scientific research methods in microwave remote sensing, density distribution and neutron transport tomography techniques.
- Significant laboratory strengths for the preparation, organization and co-ordination of test experiments involving interdisciplinary teams of physicists, chemists and engineers.
- Well developed writing skills; able to work with technical writing projects in English, French and German.
- Good interpersonal and communication skills for the collaboration and teamwork required in a scientific research team.

RESEARCH ACHIEVEMENTS

- Developed optimal method to produce charge profile of atmosphere by microwave remote sensing.
- Developed optimal numerical scheme to determine density distribution in rocks by sound travel time tomography.
- Developed more efficient numerical methods to determine flow regimes and void fractions in fluid flowing in pipes by gamma densitometers.

- Pioneered neutron transport tomography technique to determine flow regimes and void fractions in fluid flowing in fuel channels.
- Developed accurate and efficient methods to solve model equations describing radiative transfer in atmosphere.
- Developed accurate and efficient methods to obtain solutions and catastrophic points for gas ignition and biomass systems.
- Developed a new method to compute lower bounds to atomic ginding energies.
- Developed procedure to circumvent problem of spurious singularities in variational methods.
- Analyzed and characterized catastrophic behaviour and range of physical solutions in heat transfer, radiative transfer and fluid flow.

EDUCATION

Ph.D. Physics, York University, Toronto, 1977
M.Sc. Physics, Queen University, Kingsfield, 1966
M.Sc. Physics, Agraa University, India, 1963

EMPLOYMENT HISTORY

Adjunct Professor, York University, Toronto, 1982–present
Senior Scientist, Canadian Nuclear Research Centre, Pinawa, 1982–1994
Scientist/Lecturer, York University, Toronto, 1979–1984
Research Associate, University of Eastern Ontario, 1974–1979

PROFESSIONAL LEADERSHIP

Publication: Over fifty research publications in refereed journals; presentation of papers at conference proceedings; publication of international reports (list available)
Councillor, Centre for Mathematical Sciences, CNRC
University Liaison, University of Manitoba, York, Eastern
Television Host, Community Services Television

BARBARA J. BOWES

48 Résumé Drive
Winnipeg, Manitoba
ROX 3B6

Results-oriented senior sales executive with a proven track record in the consumer products industry. Superior strengths in utilizing broad experience and creative strategies to facilitate successful completion of corporate objectives. Committed to associating with an organization which will profitably exploit my talents and energy.

KEY SKILLS

- Extensive and diverse experience gained through effectively operating in over eight major retail trade classes, from boardroom to sales floor, to effectively implement and execute corporate selling plans.
- Dynamic, creative sales and marketing strategist who excels in working with the corporate team to generate realistic and achievable objectives.
- Superior strategic planning strengths in sales and marketing with the unique ability to conceive, design and implement company internal and external programs.
- Exemplary knowledge and application of the psychological principles of selling complemented by very strong interpersonal skills which confirm my abilities as a highly effective team leader, trainer and coach.
- A pro-active, enthusiastic and high energy approach not only to company goals, but also to the daily tasks needed to achieve them. Able to build enthusiastic employee participation.
- A calculating risk taker who implements creative practical solutions for profit and sales achievement for both company and clients resulting in mutual satisfaction and long term relationships.
- A keen profit awareness not only for initiating client programs which protect company profits and produce volume, but also by preparing and managing department budgets effectively with a constant lookout for creative cost savings.

ACCOMPLISHMENTS

- Envisioned a sales strategy for a stagnant, mature product line that increased annual volume from $1.4 million to $6 million and yielded significantly increased market share at the expense of competitors.

- Through an innovative sales approach, transformed a sales department operating expenses to become proportionate to sales performance, thereby protecting corporate vulnerability in difficult economic times and at the same time contributed more than $150,000 of previous annual expense to bottom line profit.
- Consistently achieved and regularly surpassed annual sales quotas with all companies within budget resulting in consistent profitability. Frequent sales growth was achieved without benefit of new products in all major product line categories.
- Expertly managed national accounts and succeeded in significantly increasing their purchase of company product by millions of dollars annually. Achievement resulted in national awards.
- Created innovative field systems and tools which saved time, increased planning and target setting efficiency and grew productivity, including electronic data equipment and user friendly territory call schedules, field reports and easy professional sales techniques and selling formats.
- Recruited, hired, supervised, trained and developed field sales reps and managers resulting in their significant achievements such as the rise through their ranks to take greater responsibilities and contribute to the companies with whom they are now employed.

EMPLOYMENT HISTORY

NATIONAL SALES MANAGER, Ridley PenMaster Canada, Toronto, 1988–present
NATIONAL SALES MANAGER, Uniglue Limited, London, 1985–1988
MANAGER, CANADIAN SALES DEVELOPMENT, Haritz Inc., 1981–1985
DISTRICT SALES MANAGER, Dominion and Son, 1966–1981

PROFESSIONAL DEVELOPMENT/EDUCATION

Managerial Grid, Scientific Systems, USA
Phone Power, Bell/Xerox
I.M.S Instructor Program, Xerox
I.M.S, M.D.S Program, Xerox
Professional Selling Skills
Dale Carnegie Public Speaking

Bachelor of Arts, Economics, University of Winnipeg

BARBARA J. BOWES

48 Résumé Drive
Winnipeg, Manitoba
ROX 3B6

Seasoned crisis counselling and mediation professional with excellent skills in problem identification, analyses and conflict resolution. Addresses advocacy issues with a humanistic management approach. Seeking opportunity in a challenging environment.

PROFESSIONAL EXPERTISE

- Well developed interviewing, counselling, mediation and analytical skills; able to be understanding while quickly identifying client needs and issues, establishes client comfort and security, facilitates effective programs of problem resolution.
- Superior level of expertise and knowledge of community resources and support networks for education, self-improvement and family assistance which enables effective advocacy for children and families.
- Proven investigative and negotiation skills ensuring effective and appropriate crisis intervention.
- Empathetic listener with intuitive strength and rapid decision making ability.
- Solid working knowledge of client admission and release procedures including: processing, screening, interviewing, co-ordinating spaces, and working with external agencies to determine and meet client needs.
- Effective task orientation with ability to work as a team leader, able to delegate responsibility, ensure harmony, establish work priorities and schedules and address concerns of clients and staff members.
- Proficiency in report writing, public relations, staff scheduling, record keeping, program and policy development, implementation and evaluation.

ACCOMPLISHMENT

- Over a ten year period, successfully supervised and managed a diverse professional and non-professional staff of 50 during a difficult social services environment.
- Identified critical areas and developed appropriate policy, implemented, oversaw and evaluated policies and ensured policy manuals were regularly updated.
- Initiated, designed and implemented a quota list system enabling all agencies to priorize their facility usage.
- Acted as a key team member to initiate, develop and implement a Cottage Intake concept within a one year timeframe.
- Initiated a continuous process improvement environment including conducting a needs assessment, designing the program and developing and training staff.

PROFESSIONAL DEVELOPMENT/EDUCATION

Bachelor of Arts, Psychology, University of Canada
Certificate, Group Facilitation, Community Services Association

Working with Victims of Abuse
Stress Management
Non Physical Crisis Intervention
Assertiveness Training

EMPLOYMENT HISTORY

STAFF MANAGER, Green Leaf Centre, Community Services, 1982–1993
SUPERVISOR, Intake Cottage, Green Leaf Centre, Community Services. 1979–1982
CLASSROOM TEACHER, Arts and Crafts, City Oaks School Division
JUVENILE COUNSELLOR, Summer Program, City Oaks School Division

BARBARA J. BOWES

48 Résumé Drive
Winnipeg, Manitoba
ROX 3B6

A challenge-oriented team player with a background as manager, trainer, coach and teacher in competitive sport and educational environments. Proven track record of success in leading and managing large sports events on a provincial and national basis. Seeking new career opportunities.

PROFESSIONAL EXPERTISE

- A strong learner-centred trainer, coach and motivator.
- Experienced at identifying training needs, designing and implementing individual as well as group training programs and measuring results.
- Excellent verbal and written communication skills with experience in public speaking and promotional, education and policy writing.
- A resourceful administrator, effective at managing multi-level projects, defining organizational needs, improving structures and efficiently utilizing resources to achieve results.
- Well developed strengths in volunteer management with ability to recruit, train, motivate and supervise youth and adult volunteer teams.
- Good working knowledge of financial management, able to develop and manage an organizational and special events budget.

ACCOMPLISHMENTS

Program Development

- Initiated and co-ordinated the development of a strategic plan for the Round Robin Rowing Club and Provincial Rowing Association; managed the successful organization and growth of both programs.
- Directed extensive revisions to the National Coaching Certificate Program; designed and piloted the updated curriculum, conducted train the trainer programs, wrote training policies and procedures.

- Developed and coached numerous winning sport programs including 16 national titles which resulted in national recognition for team members.

Communication

- Wide experience researching and writing articles, reports, media releases, promotional and educational materials.
- Designed and delivered train the trainer programs and seminars to coaches, volunteers and conference attendees on a national basis.
- Co-ordinated television, radio, and newspaper coverage of all national championship events.

Administration

- Liaised with government agencies and co-ordinated grants for the provincial association which increased by 40% over a three year period.
- Managed part-time and seasonal staff and volunteer coaches; developed job descriptions, hired, trained and evaluated.

WORK HISTORY

Executive Director/Head Coach, Provincial Club Association, 1988–1993
National Program Manager, National Club Association, 1985–1988
National Team Apprentice Coach, National Club Association, 1984–1985
Classroom Teacher, Jamestown High School, 1980–1984

AWARDS AND RECOGNITION

Coach of the Year, Provincial Sports Federation
Teaching Assistantship, University of Ottawa Valley
Canadian Domestic Coach of the Year, National Sports Federation
Athlete of the Year, Ottawa Valley High School

EDUCATION/PROFESSIONAL DEVELOPMENT

Business Management Forum, Federal Business Development Bank, 1992
National Coach Seminar, Level 1–6, Coaching Association of Canada
Masters of Arts, History, University of Ottawa Valley, 1984
Bachelor of Arts, History, University of Concord, 1982

Notes